When We Were Young

When We Were Young

By Mary Earle Gould

Illustrations By Linda Sinecola

South Brunswick and New York: A. S. Barnes and Company
London: Thomas Yoseloff Ltd

A. S. Barnes and Co., Inc.
Cranbury, New Jersey 08512

Thomas Yoseloff Ltd
108 New Bond St.
London W. 1, England

SBN: 498–06781–5
Printed in the United States of America

Dedicated to the memory of my father,
DR. JOHN WILLIAMS GOULD

FOREWORD

MARY EARLE GOULD'S POPULARITY WITH THE READING PUBLIC DERIVES in good measure from her own contagious enthusiasm about small household properties. She collected and thought about kitchen tools, boxes, cookie molds and bowls. In her mind was re-created the social and economic scene, and in imagination the bowls became filled with fruit or bread stuffing, the boxes were filled with sugar and spices and candles, the sifters and jugs and pans and jars were in the mind's eye put to use. These were the tools that made work easier, and sometimes a pleasure in the eighteenth and nineteenth centuries of this country's history.

Miss Gould's book on woodenware was published at a time when no cohesive writing on the subject was available for the non-specialist. Through her own intent interest Miss Gould set up a sounding board, and people became aware of woodenware as social history material, as well as objects with beautiful form.

Over a period of years Miss Gould has written short articles for the *Worcester Telegram* which deal with the household and the way it was run a century ago. These articles have been gathered into this book. The author jokes with and teases us with her bits of folklore. She draws in our minds a series of sketches of people, their homes, their streets, the shops, the farms, the dances. She tells in miniature bits of nineteenth-century life which touch the sentimental heart. What gown and ornaments a lady wore to a dance are just as important in this aura as election issues are to the political historian.

In arousing interest in country houses, tinware and wooden utensils Miss Gould has whetted the appetite of the collector, and done a service to dealer and museum curator alike. Surely, the gathering of information on all levels is spurred to greater heights by the efforts of such authors as Miss Gould who put their researches into print for the public to read. We thank them.

JANET R. MACFARLANE
Director
Albany Institute of History and Art

PREFACE

IN THE SPRING OF 1951, I CHANCED TO READ A SHORT STORY IN OUR daily paper that told of some romantic incident half a century back. It struck a spark in my imagination and I said to myself, "I think I can do something like that!"

My mind wandered back to the days when the various peddlers came to our back door. I mentally wrote my story and lived with it for several days. Then onto paper went "Peddlers Today and Peddlers Yesterday." Aunt Betsy the old colored bluing woman, the one-arm man who sold sewing silk and many others who knocked on our back door all came to life for me. This opened a new channel for my writing.

My first interest in writing came in 1934, and three books are to my credit—*Early American Wooden Ware, The Early American House,* and *Antique Tin and Tole Ware*—all based on my collection of woodenware, iron ware and tinware. My collection now numbers over 1200 pieces and is in the third floor of our old house. As I photographed the pieces and wrote articles for magazines, I was inspired to write my books.

It is an interesting story to tell of my becoming a collector and a writer in middle life. I taught piano as a profession, and gave lectures, performed and wrote music, along with my studying. In 1933 I changed my third-floor bedroom from one of a mid-Victorian period to one entirely of an early period. I bought a beautiful maple four-post bed and a pine dressing table. I found heirloom furniture in our storeroom which I had refinished—chairs and a chest of drawers. A rare camphor wood chest, pictures, mirrors, Mother's baby rocking chair and my doll's bed with many small family knickknacks made a most interesting room. Braided rugs came to my mind. I found piece boxes in our storeroom and began to cut strips. The next question was where to put my strips. Up country when antiquing one day, I spied a cheese box on the rafters of an old shed. It took a second trip to buy it. I had it scraped of its old green paint, leaving the initials on it intact, and placed it on my camphor wood chest.

Stroking the box as I saw it from day to day, I found myself wondering about those old wooden pantry boxes. My next find was a small oval spice box and then I found a long oval meal box on a bookcase in a home, almost concealed by dust. By the time I had twenty-seven boxes, all different, I was interviewed by our daily paper and had a page-long write-up. This brought many telephone calls and I was asked into homes to buy, which was the beginning of trips to many pantries, sheds and barns.

The late Lewis Wiggins asked me to write for the New York *Sun* and I must admit my first attempts were somewhat crude. I was told the field of woodenware was untouched. I wrote for several magazines, also, always with pictures of my pieces as illustrations. The ordeal of learning to take outdoor pictures was very exacting, but my determination carried me through.

My first book, *Early American Wooden Ware,* appeared in 1942. All the visits to old homes made me conscious of the huge fireplaces and the iron utensils and implements. I added iron ware to my pieces of woodenware, through many chance opportunities. It was then that I was asked to write a book on fireplaces and iron ware. I continued to explore old houses from cellar to attic, through darkness and cobwebs to unbearable heat, studying the construction and taking pictures. That second book appeared in 1949: *The Early American House.*

Tinware fascinated me and many rare pieces went into my collection. Again I was asked to write a book, on tinware, making a series of wood, iron, and tin. *Antique Tin and Tole Ware* appeared in the late fall of 1957. The ordeal of finding a publisher, after the first one ceased, of editing, correcting, and waiting took a lot of patience. A most necessary requisite in writing!

My research work for those three books demanded accuracy, even though I told much in a romantic vein. This collection of short stories is a sharp contrast to my other work and they are full of romance as well as historical facts. You may well know I am happy as I tell of those other days. Writing about those days and living with the stories has been sheer enjoyment. Wherever I go, I find there is a story I can write, giving it a background of my early research and my memories.

We are not living in the past when we find happiness in reminiscing. We are making the present way of living less tense and a little less hard. As you read, share with me the joy found in these stories.

I wish to acknowledge my appreciation to the Worcester *Telegram,* a daily paper, and *Feature Parade,* the Sunday magazine, in publishing these stories from time to time.

As I pick up the stories again in 1967, I realize how Time moves on;

it counts up to thirty-four years since my first box gave me an incentive for research. This year seems to hold many important happenings.

My three books have gone into second editions and this year will see *The Early American Barn*. Beyond that there should be two more books.

My collection on my top floor of 1200 pieces, valued at $50,000, has been loaned to the Shaker Village at Hancock, Massachusetts, one of the first settlements of the Shakers.

Becoming National and International through the spreading of my books, I have correspondence across the country, giving me much happiness and faith in myself. I will continue to write and continue to share my research of those long years. My autobiography reads like a fairy story and will be an inspiration for others to follow.

MARY EARLE GOULD
Worcester, Massachusetts
1967

This
Certificate of Merit
proclaimed throughout the World
is awarded to

Mary Earle Gould

for DISTINGUISHED SERVICE

by her Research & Books on Historical Subjects

and is the subject of notice in volume V

Dictionary of International Biography

Chairman of the Board

London
5th March 1968

Registrar

CONTENTS

16   CONTENTS

When We Were Young

PROLOGUE: KEEP ME LIKE A CHILD

Have you still the faith of a child,
    The joys, the hopes, the dreams?
The courage and the happy ways
    And all that childhood seems?
We go along life's relentless way,
    We toil and chafe and meet all ills;
We play our part, we fill our place,
    We take what'ere God wills.
But have we lost the joys and dreams
    That made us young again?
Have we lost those care-free ways,
    As we struggle in our pain?
God grant to me those happy days
    When life was all it seems—
God grant to me those long-lost days,
    Keep me like a child with dreams.

PART I
IN THE KITCHEN

1

KITCHENS YESTERDAY, TODAY AND TOMORROW

THE DEVELOPMENT OF KITCHENS MIGHT WELL BE DIVIDED INTO THREE periods; that of the 17th and 18th centuries, that of the 19th century, and that of the 20th century.

Step into a house of the 17th century and you step into a kitchen that served as living room, workroom, and bedroom. It was called the "hall" over in England, and in this country it became the "keeping room" or the "fire room." It was a large room, extending nearly across one side of the house. It faced south, so as to have all the sun possible. You entered the room from the outdoor yard.

Pine panelling of beautifully grained, wide boards from the virgin forests extended around the room. Similar boards of as much as 20 or more inches were in the floor. The huge fireplace with its dark and cavernous opening added to the somber, subdued tone of the big room. Often those fireplaces were 11 feet long, 5 feet high, and as deep as they were high. The logs burned in such a fireplace were seven and eight feet long, dragged into the room by men with the aid of oxen.

The fire burned day and night, providing heat both for cooking and for warmth. The windows were small with small panes of imperfect glass coming from England. With a door of solid panels and windows with small panes, little light came into that room.

The sink in one corner of the room was of wood or soapstone, a substance found in the nearby soil. Its outlet was a pipe put through a hole in the wall to the outdoors. Water was brought in from a well or sometimes it was piped in from an outside stream. Scrubbing brushes were made from splintered birch saplings and home-made soap helped to make the task of scrubbing easier.

The spinning wheel and the loom were in another corner. The bed that turned up or one that stood with a trundle bed underneath was against the wall. A cradle was at one side. A cupboard to hold the few

25

A kitchen of yesterday

dishes, some of wood, stood in a corner. A table and a few stools and a bench, a high-back settle by the fireplace, and a chest or two made up the scant furnishings. Fastened to the panelling by the fireplace opening, opposite the settle, was a long, slender wooden crane. A blanket was hung on this to further keep out the cold drafts.

Cooking was done in and over the fire; roasting, broiling, and stewing. Baking was done before the fire and in the brick oven at one side of the fireplace. The early implements were back-breaking; heavy iron kettles and pots, gridirons, toasters, spiders, and skillets. All of these had their own special duties to perform. Tin reflector ovens came when tin was available and they made the work less difficult in the lifting and leaning over the hot embers.*

The second period that marked the change in the old kitchens came about when the iron cook stove or range appeared. There is very little recorded about iron cook stoves, called the cooking range. Probably it has had scant interest for later generations. One of the earliest recorded cooking ranges is the James stove made in Troy, New York, known as the Baltimore Cook Stove, patented on April 26, 1815. This was the first satisfactory stove and was in use for about 25 years.

Wood was burned in those first stoves, generally until 1851. The shaking grate was adopted by P. P. Stewart and then coal came into use. Charcoal was often used to make an intense heat, for charcoal gave out one-third more heat than wood or coal.

* The Early American House, Gould.

In Memorial Hall in Old Deerfield, Massachusetts, is an odd stove with a round revolving top. This is recorded in the American Encyclopedia as having been invented by Henry Stanley of Poultney, Vermont, in 1832. There is an oblong fire box at the front. The stove top has holes of different sizes with lids, five if I recall, to hold the different-sized pots or other utensils. The top turned about, bringing the required-sized hole over the fire. It seems a bit impractical, putting all that extra work on the housewife, of turning the heavy stove top around for the right-sized hole for each pot.

Recollections of the old kitchens of the 19th century always arouse nostalgia in the hearts of the older generations. Here, the kitchen seemed as before to be the heart of the home; that kitchen with its coal black range with shiny nickel trimmings and a teakettle singing on top.

The housewife made her doughnuts in a big iron kettle. She baked muffins, cookies, and bread in the oven, with no thermometer to register the heat. By thrusting her hand into the oven, as they did with the old brick ovens, she was able to judge the proper temperature. She baked her pots of beans every Saturday and made brown bread with raisins in a steamer on top of the stove. She cooked the Thanksgiving turkey to a perfect brown; she boiled, fried, and stewed in pots and pans. The task of removing the ashes and shovelling in coal was all in the day's work.

The children dried pumpkin seeds in the bottom oven, and when wet shoes and stockings had to be dried, they too went into that oven. On cold days, after playing outside, the children's hands reached toward the heat from the stove top. And how the men loved to open the oven door and sit with their feet inside! A mother's joy knew no bounds when the men folk and the children came into the kitchen in the evening. With the work done, they gathered there in the warmth and glow of the kitchen range. In your mind's eye you can picture the plants in the window, a bird swinging in its cage, a cat and a dog that romped at will, glass lamps with reflectors behind them swinging in holders against the wall. A rocking chair or two, a couch by the window, and a motto on the wall reading HOME SWEET HOME, done in cross stitch by industrious hands. That is what today's older generations remember, from their childhood.

Records show that gas appeared in 1890 and the price was low. Gas ranges came into kitchens, but for a long time they did not usurp the iron cook stove. Small gas stoves often stood at the end of the old stove and were used on the few occasions when it was needless to start up a coal fire. If a check could be made to find how many cook stoves are still in use, one would find many! There is nothing more wonderful than the pot of beans baked in the oven—an all-day baking. And muffins and cakes in the old iron pans are far superior to those baked in tins with gas.

And how about the iron doughnut kettle that was recently thrown out as junk? Not all of them met this fate.

In 1914, electric stoves began to be made, although they were not popular until 1920. It was not for another 25 years or more before electric stoves became attractive and ornamental to the kitchen. Today, gas ranges and electric ranges compete with each other in attractive models.

The kitchen of today would make our ancestors' eyes blink with astonishment. Could they imagine ovens in the wall, set into the chimney, gas or electric as the choice might be. An electric light within the oven makes baking or roasting visible. The switches for speeds and controls are outside the oven on the wall, below the beautiful chrome doors. There is no stooping or bending as those ancestors did generations ago while cooking in the open fireplace. A stove-top range stands at one side, with a hood over it to carry away all odors. This connects with the chimney flue which also carries away the odors of the oven.

Now Fashion decrees that kitchen ranges and refrigerators will be black instead of white. Perhaps in colors as well. Now walls are light blue or pink or yellow or perhaps green to offset the black appliances. All other equipment is shiny chrome.

Sinks are beyond description; part of the equipment is the dish pan, the other the refuse grinder. There is a button for this and a button for that; grinders, egg beaters, fruit juicers, and cake mixers. Food comes as "mixes" and the labor of mixing is nil! Cupboards replace pantry and buttery, taking little space in systematic orderliness. The refrigerator and deep freeze units take care of the food at all seasons of the year. Washing machines, dryers, and dishwashers are the rest of the mechanical devices that meet the eye in the kitchen of today.

Perhaps this generation of housewives is becoming soft, what with all the electric gadgets, and growing mentally lazy with everything done for them. It is a far cry from the open fireplace and the iron pots and kettles.

2

THE OLD KITCHEN TOOLS

TURN BACK THE PAGES OF HISTORY 50 YEARS—JUST 50 YEARS—AND you will find yourself in an age of little mechanical help in the home. It was a time when men and women labored and accomplished things with hand tools and hand gadgets.

Today there is a meat grinder with assorted blades. Half a century ago, a chopping knife could accomplish anything that needed to be chopped or ground. In my collection is an array of 70 chopping knives, all hand-made and no two alike. A piece of steel and a piece of wood were all that was needed. It was not always a sizable piece of steel. One man used a footscraper and welded a narrow piece of steel to the edge and set that into a piece of hickory sapling for a handle. Another man took a hatchet head, cut out the center, leaving two ends which he set into a wooden handle. The edge was sharpened for a chopping knife. Still another man used a small bone from a lamb's leg for a handle, shaped naturally to fit the hand.

The steel blades are of all shapes—narrow, wide, moon-shape, and sickle-shape, with a curved or a straight edge. The handles, too, vary, as each man used what wood he had on hand. One handle was set at right angles to the blade, giving a different purchase. There are some chopping knives with a double blade and some with three blades extending from the handle. Two of the knives have crossed blades.

Every household had a wooden chopping bowl. They were round or oblong, of many shapes and sizes. Into those went the stuff to be chopped. Meat for hash, meat for sausages, vegetables for stews, cucumbers and tomatoes for pickling. It was muscle and the chopping knife that did the work. Today we buy hash, all prepared, soup with vegetables diced and pickles of all varieties. All with no effort on our part. We are losing our muscle.

Another hand tool was the grater made of tin. They were made from

29

a sheet of tin, pierced full of holes made with a nail when the tin was placed on a piece of wood. The sheet was then nailed to a board back with a protruding handle. One of mine is dated Feb. 1794.

The small graters were for nutmegs. Nutmegs came to this country when whaling vessels went out to other lands and returned with spices in their hold, among various other things. In my museum is a tall glass jar of nutmegs, preserved in alcohol. Dating back over 150 years, they were brought back by a sea captain. Nutmegs are covered with an outer shell, looking much like a smooth chestnut burr. Over the nutmeg in the shell is a lacey covering which was mace. The nutmegs were stripped of the mace and both spices were left to dry before using; the nutmeg grated and the mace powdered.

Nutmeg graters are of all sizes and constructions. One in the family was slender, about four inches long with a pocket at the end for the nutmeg. There is a tiny one less than two inches long. It has a little tin holder for the nutmeg, with a tiny cover that opens with a hinge. The sides are the grater. This was used to carry in the vest pocket when a man went to see a neighbor. It was a social neighbor who always served drinks at his fireside; flip or hot toddy. The tiny grater held forth when the owner flavored his own drink with the nutmeg grater, as he liked it. In some Art Museums there are small silver nutmeg graters that performed the service like the tin ones.

The largest of the tin graters measure about 15 inches long; a curved,

Old pantry tools

pierced sheet of tin nailed to a board back. In the early days, butter was colored to offset its paleness. That was in the winter months when there was not sufficient goodness in the hay. Carrots were grated to produce a juice used to give a deeper color to the butter. But a law was eventually made to penalize such a practice.

The housewives made their own yeast from raw potatoes. The raw potatoes were grated on a tin grater and some handy man decided it was quicker work to use two hands with two potatoes on a large grater. Potatoes were also grated and made into starch. Cheese was grated as it is today and used in cooking. It took muscle to use a tin grater for the many things that had to be grated.

Every family had one or more mortar and pestle in the kitchen. They have now been relegated to the top shelf or else sold to collectors. A mortar and pestle was necessary in many ways. Salt came to the home in coarse form and had to be pounded fine. Sugar was either maple or white sugar that was sold in a tall pyramid form, wrapped in purple paper. That had to be broken and powdered in a mortar with a pestle. Spices such as mace, cinnamon, bark, whole cloves, whole peppers, and ginger root all had to be pounded to a powder before they could be used. That took muscle.

Long ago, a small birch broom was used to beat eggs and cream. Then came the metal beaters. Remember the one that was shaped like a hoop skirt, with coils of wire around a wooden handle? You pressed it down and it jumped back—it was like a Punch and Judy show. That contraption beat eggs, whipped cream, and mashed and whipped potatoes. Then came the egg beaters with two sets of blades that worked with a crank on a wheel. I still use one to keep my muscles in trim.

Long ago, we had a wire beater that was fastened to the wall. The arms were long loops of wire which revolved with a crank. A deep, square glass holder came with it. You held the glass with the eggs or cream with the wire arms down in the mixture. Turning the crank beat them quickly with slight effort. Today, it is an electric beater and mixer.

There is an electric juicer, too. The early method of extracting the juice from lemons was really ridiculous. A corrugated knob on a handle, of wood or sometimes of china, was thrust into the core of half a lemon. You had to guide the lemon juice so it would not squirt where you did not want it to go. Then about 75 years ago, someone invented a squeezer with two wooden arms hinged. On one arm was a hollow the size of a lemon that had holes in it and on the other was a mound the size of half a lemon. You laid the lemon half over the hollow, flat side down, pressed the two arms together and the juice ran down through the holes. There is a long squeezer that was used, laid onto a tub at picnics. The holes were at one side so the juice flowed down into the tub. Someone put their small juicer on legs so the tumbler could be placed underneath the holes and catch the juice. Someone went still better and put two knife blades at the end to cut the lemon before squeezing it. Today, it is an electric juicer!

Why apple parers were discarded is something to be figured out. The first ones were wooden with a thin knife blade on a handle, which was held in the hand. Some were made to fasten to the table, one was made on the end of a small four-legged bench on which the worker sat as he pared, bushel after bushel. Another one was at the end of a plank with a round end on which the worker sat. Others were held in the lap, made on a large or small plank. Wheels, pulleys, and a crank make up the ingenious apple parer of wood. A three-point prong held the apple and the worker turned the crank backwards, working toward him. Holding the knife in his hand, he guided it as the apple lost its skin row by row. Iron parers were invented by the middle of the 19th century. These screwed to the table. One style pared the apple around once and then snapped back to begin another row. It was all done by turning a crank.

There were stirrers, skimmers, scoops, spatulas, rolling pins, gingerbread prints, and cooky rollers. There were butter prints and butter molds and sausage guns for making sausages. All of this woodenware was found in the old kitchens, made by the handyman or the cooper.

We are saving much time in this "push button" age. Perhaps we are growing soft!

3

WHAT'S HAPPENING TO THE KITCHEN SINK?

AN EDITORIAL BROUGHT UP THE KITCHEN SINK FOR DISCUSSION. IT IS GO-
ing to take the center of the stage in the plans of modern plumbing and be
placed in the middle of the kitchen. Community houses and many such
places where the public meets for social activities have for quite some
time put the sink in the middle of their remodeled kitchens.

If our ancestors should come back and see our modern kitchens with
modern plumbing, it would be like Rip Van Winkle coming back from
his long sleep of 20 years and finding the old ways changed.

The question of plumbing was impossible when the Pilgrim Fathers
built their first homes. The kitchen was large, the center of the house,
with its cavernous fireplace and small-paned windows. Water was brought
from a nearby stream or a well in wooden buckets. All washing and family ablutions were performed in wooden tubs and wooden basins. Rainwater from a barrel that stood at the corner of the house under a wooden
spout helped ease the need of water.

The first underground pipes for bringing water into the house were
made of wooden logs, with a hole in the center bored by means of a
tool called a reamer. Wood deteriorated from water and insects and the
pipes did not last many years. Then soapstone was discovered in the soil
as a working material and made into small, square-edged pipes.

The first sinks were made of wood. One is like a table with slat legs,
a four-inch rim around the edge and a hole bored in one corner for the
water to run through. It is painted, except in the inside, that lovely old
blue; the paint is made from the indigo plant. This stood by a window in
the kitchen or sometimes in the large pantry. Water was brought to the
sink in buckets and another bucket stood on the floor under the sink to
catch the water when it ran through the hole.

The next experiment with the kitchen sink was with soapstone. Soapstone sinks are sometimes found today in old houses. They are really

33

beautiful for their color, shape, and smoothness—worn down by many generations. They are large in size, with deep slanting sides, a hole in one corner in the bottom and a holder for the homemade cake of soap in another corner, made in one piece with the sink. At Plymouth, Massachusetts, in the old Harlow House, the sink has a channel that leads outdoors, through the wall, so the water could flow out after it had been used. This saved the use of a bucket. Being very heavy, soapstone sinks were propped up on supports. Soapstone wears smooth in the course of time, but these sinks never wore out.

An ingenious way of supplying water for the sink was to pipe it from a nearby stream. If possible, houses were built by a stream or where water could be obtained from a well. In an old house in Colrain, not far from Greenfield, Massachusetts, there is a soapstone sink with its water supplied by a pipe from a stream running under the house. For many generations, the flow of water has never ceased; cold, sparkling water. Another such stream piped into a sink is on the outskirts of Worcester, where our family used to vacation. There must be many more.

Another generation saw iron sinks. These were manufactured by a foundry and fitted into a built-in frame. With the iron sinks came pumps, also a manufactured product, bringing water from an outdoor well. Iron sinks rusted and never brought any joy to the housewife.

Today's beautiful arrangement of the kitchen is beyond any dream the housewife in the days of the Pilgrim Fathers might have had. The

What's happening to the Kitchen Sink?

enamel sink with its shiny chrome faucets and most artistically fashioned soap holders and outlets, with its twin set tub at one side, is the result of skilled designers.

The future may give us a sink in the middle of the kitchen, but one thing would be greatly missed—the view from the window over the sink.

4

YESTERDAY'S SOAPMAKING

THE COMMON SOAPS AND SOAP POWDERS OF TODAY HAVE DEVELOPED through a long process beginning soon after the birth of Christ. Pliny the great historian tells of soap in his writings in the year 23 A.D. And excavations of Pompeii brought to light a complete soap-making establishment and the finding of well-preserved soap.

The soap of those earliest years was made from tallow of goat's fat mixed with lye from the ashes of beech trees.

In Early Colonial America, domestic animals were seldom slaughtered for meat and fats, because milk, butter, and cheese were more important foods. When the herds increased, the animals could be spared, and meat, hides, and hoofs that went into the making of a binder for paint were taken from the slaughtered animals. Then fat accumulated which could be used in making soap.

The fat was saved all winter and the ashes from the fireplace and the bake oven were kept; these are the two ingredients for making soap. When autumn came with clear, cool days, the fat was "tried out" in the great iron kettles hanging on the crane, and the result was clear grease or tallow.

The next task was to make the lye. Out in the yard was a large stone, three feet in diameter, into which had been cut a circle larger than the bottom of the barrel. From the circle, a channel led to the outer edge. The stone was set on a sloping spot so a tub could be placed under the front edge. A barrel was placed on the stone. Into the barrel went a layer of straw, a layer of ashes, repeated until the barrel was two-thirds full. Rainwater had been caught for many months in the rain barrel, at the corner of the house under the eaves spout, for rain water is considered to be very pure and soft. For three days, water was added to the ashes and straw, and as it trickled through to the groove and into the tub it became lye. If it was the proper strength, an egg or a potato would float in it. If the egg or potato sank, the lye was not strong enough and more water had to be poured through the ashes.

The process of making lye was called leaching, the barrel was called a leach barrel and the stone on which the barrel rested was a leaching stone. A few of the old stones can be found today, used as doorstones or steps, and they are highly prized. Six bushels of ashes and twenty-four pounds of grease went into the process of making soap, taking an entire day.

A huge iron pot, measuring as much as three feet in diameter, was swung on poles out in the yard and a hot fire was started underneath. Into the kettle went the grease and the lye. The mess was stirred with a wooden paddle made of sassafras wood, which gave a pleasing odor, cutting that of the grease. These spatulas, now in museums, are bleached from contact with the lye. If the mess was the right consistency, the soap would "come." If not, more lye was added. It was a proud housewife whose soap turned out well. Soft soap like jelly was the result. It was put into a barrel and when needed, it was ladled out with a square-sided wooden scoop made from a block of wood. Scoops, too, were bleached from the lye in the soap.

By the middle of the 17th century, hard soap began to be made. Around 1850, hard soap was made by adding resin for oil which made the soap hard and potash which made the soap whiter. In the early days, a fragrant soap was made from the wax of bayberries. It took a bushel of berries to make four or five pounds of soap.

Before the turn of the 20th century, a soap that floated was accidentally discovered. A workman in a soap factory left the kettle boiling when he went off for his lunch hour, and upon returning found the batch full of air bubbles. Without realizing at the time that this would make the soap float, he considered his mistake a calamity. But it proved to be one of those accidents that ended in a discovery.

Quite often in the old days there was a soap shop, a small building in the yard. Small shops housed shoemakers, cobblers, blacksmiths, and coopers or woodturners, taking such labor away from the kitchen. In the soap shop, the kettle was not suspended over a fire. Instead, a four-sided brick frame was made on which rested the rim of the kettle; the kettle was set down into the frame high enough for a fire to be built underneath. Here were brought the wood ashes and the barrel of clarified grease or tallow. And here stood barrels of the finished soft soap, ready to be used by the family and to be peddled on trips to other towns.

In a small town near Worcester, the late Francis Howard Drake, of East Brookfield, was the third generation in his family to make soap and candles. He himself ceased active manufacture many years ago, turn-

Yesterday's soapmaking

ing his farm into a market garden and using the soap shop for a sales room. His grandfather, born in 1808, had a house in the center of the town and land on the North Brookfield road, a short distance away. On this "farm" he built a soap shop and began to make soap and candles as a trade. In 1872, the grandfather built a house and barn on the farm and went there to live. His son, Arthur Howard Drake, and grandson, the late Mr. Drake, both lived on the farm.

On the brow of a banking in the side yard once stood a soap shop. The foundation can still be seen, tumbled in and covered with dirt and weeds. At the foot of the banking was the cellar of the shop, with a big iron door. The huge iron pot measured three feet across and two and one half feet high, resting in the three-sided brick frame or oven. It was held by two ears so the pot could be tilted. The old pot continued to do duty by holding ashes from the kitchen stove.

Here in his cellar, the soap was made from wood ashes and fat and bones brought back from the peddling trips. Here the candles were made, the tallow first purified in the big pot and then poured into molds which held the wicks of twisted tow.

On the upper level of the shop was a big storage room, its wide door opening onto the driveway. The barrels of soft soap and finished candles packed into wooden boxes were loaded onto a wagon drawn by two horses. The grandfather went to the neighboring towns to peddle. He sold not only to the housewives but to several shoemakers. Shoemakers used soap in the process of tanning leather and they needed candles by which to work. Every small town had its shoemaker and its cobbler, which were as necessary as the blacksmith and the wheelwright.

On the return trip, the wagon held barrels filled with ashes, fat, and bones. Very little money was used in those days, the transaction being done by swapping—so much soap or so many candles for so much grease or fat or bones. Dinnertime often found the grandfather eating with the family as a welcome guest.

The grandfather went on his trips alone, leaving his son to tend the kettle in the shop. One day, the fire was either too hot or the kettle was too full, for the mess overflowed and caught fire. The son, alone on the job, could not check the flames and the shop burned down. This was in 1865. A second shop was built.

About 1870 the soft soap changed to hard soap; the process called for alum and resin. The grandfather and then the son made the long trip to Boston with oxen to buy these chemicals.

The son took over the business and had with him his son, the late owner of the farm on the North Brookfield road. After the father's death, (the second generation) Francis Howard Drake turned his attention to a market garden. The soap shop, the second one to be erected, was moved to the opposite side of the house and became a house for vegetables and melons.

Ledgers and bills among Mr. Drake's possessions date back to 1856. Bills dated 1868 and 1872 show that money began to enter into the transaction. It lists a barrel of soap—written "bbl"—at $6. In exchange is grease and tallow, which went for about 8½ cents a pound, taken away in some sort of a bag. Subtracting the stock, or the grease and the tallow, the bill was very small. Oxen were "let out," too, according to the bill, at $2 for a half day.

Today, a cake of soap can be very refreshing. There are so many scents to choose from, to suit the most capricious whims. And the cakes take many forms in many colors. Even the boxes the cakes come in are made to attract the eye. There is a bath mitt that slips onto the hand and a ball of soap that has a cord that goes around the neck so the ball cannot slip away and be lost in the water. Children have their pet animal shapes to tempt them to use soap and water. There are colors to match the scheme of the bath room; lavender, green, gold, yellow, and blue.

Not too many years ago, in the Gay Nineties, it was Pears' soap that was the attraction. A wonderful advertisement met the eye, picturing glamorous women and jaunty men. "Good morning! Have you used Pears' Soap?" If you did not use Pears' soap you had a guilty feeling and straightway went out and purchased a cake. "No other soap in the world is used so much, and so little goes so far."

Then there was an advertisement for Wool Soap. Two little curly haired girls in their undershirts are standing together. The shirt of one of them is long and unspoiled by laundering. On the other, the shirt has shrunk badly. "My mama used Wool soap," says one of the tiny tots.

"I wish mine had," says the other.

Pearline was the most popular washing powder in the Gay Nineties. The clothes cried out in an advertisement; "Wash us with Pearline. Don't experiment on us with imitations. We'd rather be rubbed to pieces than be eaten up."

Many housewives are making their own soap today. A can of lye from the store shelf and clarified fat from leftover scraps, a large shallow pan and a wooden spoon make up the outfit needed. Today's housewives are making soap that floats and they sometimes scent it and use it for the toilet. It is a proud housewife who views her rows of white soap stocked on a pantry shelf or stored in a drawer or cupboard away from the light.

It is a far cry from the soap of our grandmothers and great-grandmothers to the white soap of the modern housewife and to the commercial soaps and powders put out by manufacturers.

5

THE LOWLY POTATO IS MAKING NEWS

POTATOES CAME FROM CHILE TO MEXICO AND THENCE UP TO VIRGINIA. From Virginia, they went to Ireland and thence to England. Sir Walter Raleigh was the first to cultivate them extensively, on his estates in Cork, Ireland. Then the Scotch-Irish settlers of New Hampshire, when visiting their native Ireland, brought some back to this country, where they acquired the name of "Irish potatoes."

The name potato came from the old word *batata* and other names sprung up for them: taters, spuds, tubers. Tuber applies to the potato because they grow at the end of the plant as a root. They have "eyes" in them and these eyes were called "balls" by the early Colonists; they were the part that was eaten.

In New England, the potato was not promoted until 1750. It was believed that if anyone ate potatoes every day, they could not survive seven years. And if potatoes were left over from one season, they were burned in the belief that cattle or horses would die if they ate them.

An account says that a popular way of cooking potatoes was with butter, sugar, and grape juice, mixed with dates, lemons and the spice mace; then seasoned with cinnamon, nutmeg and sugar; then covered with a frosting of sugar! That sounds to us like a pudding and it is little wonder that potatoes were not considered a vegetable.

In some section, the potatoes were cut in chunks, dried in the oven, and hung up in bags. When needed, the pieces were roasted, ground in a mill or powdered in a mortar and pestle. This was used as coffee.

The real batata or potato was the sweet potato. This grew in the warm climes in the South. They were roasted or boiled and were used in puddings and in bread or even in pancakes. They had the taste of almonds according to records in old diaries.

Raw potatoes were used in making starch and yeast. They were grated on tin graters, those early ones being a sheet of pierced tin which was

The lowly potato is making news

nailed to a shaped slab of wood, with a protruding handle. Every household had these tin graters of all sizes. One in my museum measures 20 inches long on a slab of wood six inches wide. The tin curves away from the board to give space for the gratings to go through. With a long grater, a potato could be held in each hand with the board lying flat on a table. The job would be done twice as quickly as when the grater was held in one hand and a potato was grated with the other.

Starch was made by putting the grated potatoes through a sieve and cooking them with water. The mixture was stirred with a wooden paddle. The potato starch settled to the bottom, the water poured off, and the layer of starch thoroughly dried. This was washed again and dried. It was then ready for use.

Yeast in the old days was liquid. Part of the batch was saved in an earthen crock from one generation to another, from grandmother to mother to daughter, a little of the old used each time the new was made. It was a combination of potatoes, salt and hops, or settlings of beer barrels. The important property of yeast was something fermented.

Today, potatoes are as important a food as bread, even though bread has been called the "staff of life." Although they once grew wild in the soil, potatoes are now highly cultivated, with several varieties in the market.

6

A BOWL OF HOT FISH CHOWDER

FROM MY CHILDHOOD I HAVE ALWAYS WANTED TO KNOW HOW THINGS were done. I used to watch the men-folk carpenter and Mother or the maid cook. Little wonder that I am not afraid to try anything that comes along!

When it came to cooking, one thing especially was impressed upon my mind and that was how to make fish chowder. It came time for me to take over; I was no longer a child. I was amazed at my ability to remember, without books or instruction, how to make fish chowder. Just from watching Mother! To be told that it was as good or better than that of my Mother's was high praise!

This will sound like a rule from a cookbook. First I "try out" thin slices of salt pork under the broiler. I place a pan of water over a flame. I pare my potatoes and cut them into thin slices, leaving them standing in water. Then I pour the fat from the pork into a large saucepan. I put in a layer of the pared potatoes and sprinkle it well with salt and flour from a flour shaker. I put in part of the haddock fillet—it could be a small fish with bones and skin or just fillet slices. Some say the skin and bones give a rich flavor. I salt the fish and sprinkle it with flour. Next comes another layer of potatoes sprinkled well with salt and flour and another layer of fish sprinkled well. Onion slices can be put in but our family does not add them. The fish and potatoes are covered with the water that has been simmering in a pan. "Put in enough water until it is in sight." With a large three-tined fork, I lift the potatoes and fish away from the bottom of the kettle to be sure the mixture does not burn.

When the potatoes are about done, I scatter in common crackers that have been split and soaked in water a few minutes. Next, I pour in milk and put in some butter—a "generous piece!" Another short cooking and the cook tastes to know what she has made. The flour from the shaker

43

A bowl of hot fish chowder

thickens the milk with just the right consistency and the pork pieces and liquid plus the additional butter give just the right richness.

Imagine my surprise when I looked in my grandmother's cookbook of 1846 and found the rule for chowder was exactly as I had been making it! From grandmother to mother to daughter! Instead of a saucepan, it was a dinner pot; instead of milk, it was a teacup of cream. No butter was added, as the pork seemed sufficient.

In 1954, reports from the Fishery Trade Associaton told that more than 15 million pounds of haddock fillets were on hand in this country. The Secretary of the Interior put out a plea that more fillet be consumed. The so-called "haddock belt" includes the Northeastern and North-central states and extends as far as North Carolina.

At the same time, a report came that a king crab had been found in Alaska, weighing 12 pounds with arms five feet from tip to tip. That seems to be reverting back to the old days when the Pilgrims came to this country. Lobsters weighed 25 pounds apiece and were often five and six feet long. One lobster made a meal for a family. One crab was large enough to satisfy the appetite of four men. Oysters, too, were large, a foot in length, and they were either roasted on gridirons or pickled and put away in the larder in crocks of earthernware.

As to the codfish, they literally filled the waters on the coast of New England. This gave the promontory of Massachusetts the name of Cape Cod. When a man went fishing, he was allowed only the fish he caught "on his own hook," which brought about that expression. Young boys helped and learned the trade. They had to cut the tails of each fish they caught to claim possession. All seacoast towns set up large fleets of fishing boats.

What is so wonderful as a bowl of hot fish chowder on a cold winter's day!

7

BREAD, THE STAFF OF LIFE

"ABOUT 40,000,000 LOAVES OF BREAD ARE SOLD IN THE UNITED STATES every day." So reports the Associated Press.

Our ancestors had no such help in the old days. With large families to feed and large ovens in which to bake, they made their own bread. Rye meal and "injun" meal was all they had at first.

As proof of the amount of bread that was made, there's a large tub in my museum, over two feet across and 20 inches deep. The inside is still white with stains of flour. This tub came from a family nearby to Worcester. There is a large oblong box, too, called a dough trough or dough tray—dotray for short. A long paddle for stirring and a long thin knife for cutting the dough into loaves hang on the wall, both of wood and both a yard long. The batch of dough must have made about 20 loaves.

The dough tray box had slanting sides, and a cover set inside. A little ways down at either end were two small notches, in which rested a long, narrow stick called a lintel or temse. When the flour was sifted into the mixture, the sieve rested on this stick and was moved back and forth. The old saying of "setting the Thames on fire" came from a fear that the friction of the wooden sieve rim might start a spark on the wooden temse—temse changed to Thames in the saying. Sticks are generally missing, for they were merely a stick of wood and became kindling. And covers are missing, and more than that the old dough trays now serve as holders for kindling wood by an open fire!

An old rule from the historic town of Deerfield, Massachusetts, dates back 100 years. It says: "Put a bushel of good flour into a trough; mix with it two gallons of warm water and three pints of good yeast; put it into the flour and stir well with your hands till it becomes tough. Let it rise and then add another two gallons of warm water and a pound of salt. Work it well, cover it with a cloth." (Was the cover missing?)

45

It had to rise again. "Make your loaves about five or six pounds each, clean your oven and put in your bread; shut it closed and bake three hours."

The oven was the big brick oven, first heated by building a fire within and if the housewife could hold her hand inside and count up to 30, the oven was hot enough. Then the embers were swept out and dried oak leaves or cabbage leaves were placed on the bottom in lieu of any pans. The loaves were put in with a long-handled wooden bread peel or shovel, first sprinkled with cornmeal.

The Bible says that bread was made in the form of thin cakes, baked on the hearth or in a brick oven. Often, they were made with oil instead of butter and either leavened or unleavened—with or without yeast. Even in the time of Moses, leaven was used in making bread. It is said that the Egyptians were the first to use leaven; that the secret afterwards became known to the Greeks; that the Greeks communicated it to the Romans who spread the invention far and wide in the Northern countries.

The South in Colonial times made hoe cakes, so-called because the hard, flat cakes were baked on the head of a hoe in front of the fire, with the handle out in the room. The North had similar cakes or bread baked on a board propped up in front of the fire, called bannock cakes. The board often had a prop of its own and was called a bannock board. The South had spoon bread and beaten biscuit, peculiar to that section. Beaten bread was made by beating and kneading the dough for a long period. A correspondent in Texas tells me of having a beaten biscuit table much over 100 years old, made from a tree on a plantation in Kentucky. As the table became rough and worn from use, it was smoothed down and polished again. At the present time, it is four inches thick although several layers of wood have been taken off. Another correspondent in Texas tells of having a beaten biscuit hole punch, something I could not describe. Still another person in Kentucky wanted me to buy a worker, all wood, which appears to have been a table with a roller attached to it which beat and rolled the dough.

Our family had a large tin bread pan, the size of a dish pan, but with a low standard and cover. I can still see those loaves of bread with their crispy brown crusts! Part of the dough was saved out to be made into fried bread doughnuts for Sunday morning breakfast, eaten with maple syrup! Remember those fried bread doughnuts? I learned to make bread and rolls and had a patent mixer that screwed to the table. It had a crank that turned the double-looped arm that mixed the dough. Some of those mixers are still being used for I see requests for them in magazine advertisements. They did a good job of stirring and kneading.

Remember the round, flat wooden bread boards that were used on the table to hold a loaf of bread? How collectors hunt for them! A friend is collecting them and has a row of them on a plate rail in her kitchen. Some have an inscription around the edge, decorated with a spray of wheat and a leaf. Mine have Spare Not, The Staff of Life and Bread. There used to be a knife with a wooden handle with the inscription BREAD on it. I have but recently had one given to me. A steel knife called a Christy Bread Knife was very popular at one time. It had a scalloped edge to facilitate cutting. With it came a slender cake knife. Bread was cut at the table on a bread board with the wide Christy knife. I remember when I visited my Aunt Abbie how she cut a slice of bread on the board and passed it on the knife for us to reach. I wonder where that board is now!

Bread, the staff of life

A small wooden dish that held butter under a glass dome with BUTTER stamped on the rim was a rare find for me at an auction. Even at that, a friend has one on his top pantry shelf now. But most of these things went out as kindling wood. How often we say, "I wonder what became of that!"

Bread and jam, bread and molasses, bread and gravy, or plain bread and butter, home-made from sweet cream! From the beginning, civilized man has had his bread in one form or another—the staff of life.

8

CRACKERS AND BISCUITS

SOME FRIENDS OF MINE BOUGHT AN OLD HOUSE IN EXETER, NEW HAMP-
shire, dating back more than 200 years. When exploring the many re-
cesses and sealed sections, they discovered a bricked-up oven in the cellar.

Upon opening it, they found what they believed to be a cracker oven.
A flue went up into the main chimney and it was disclosed that the heat
came from a pot of charcoal. An iron pot was still in the oven, partly
filled with charcoal as mute evidence of the use of the oven. While the
crackers were baking, live charcoal had to be burning continuously until
the batch was done. Five fireplaces in the house supplied the charcoal
during the process. Charcoal, burnt embers of maple or birch wood, was
used for crackers because it gave out twice as much heat as any other fuel
and it never broke into a flame.

There is a modern cracker factory north of Worcester. The oven
below the floor level has a temperature of 450 degrees for its baking. A
huge roller like a ferris wheel has four suspending arms on which lies
the cracker dough, stamped in blocks. The wheel revolves, carrying the
dough on the arms down into the heat and up again. After passing through
the heat a certain number of revolutions, the crackers are ready to be
taken off. They are removed with a long-handled wooden shovel, the
perfect ones separated from the broken ones.

The word cracker means a flat, hard biscuit which in turn means a
flat bread made dry and hard by baking for preservation. There are many
variations of the word biscuit of the old days. Sea bread or sea biscuit,
ship biscuit and Captain's biscuit lead us to believe that those early biscuits
were made for ships that went out to sea. Still another name was pilot
biscuit or pilot bread, which became the well-known pilot cracker. Sailors
were on board ship many months at a time and such food as those biscuit-
crackers could be taken on the journey. In my research work on tin and

48

preserving in tin, I have discovered that food was preserved in tins and sent out on ships as early as 1806.

The ingredients of these biscuits with the various names were wheaten flour, water, and salt. Captain's biscuit had a little butter and a little yeast added. Hard-tack, still another name for those biscuits, we associate with soldiers rather than sailors. In my collection is a hard-tack cracker claimed to have been made in the days of the Civil War. And there are two rolling pins with projections that rolled out the dough. A cracker stamp has a set of five metal headless nails on a handle and was used in making the holes. The biscuit crackers were square but the pilot crackers were round.

Crackers and biscuits

There are three tin biscuit ovens in my collection, each one heated by charcoal. One has a removable pot with a wire handle which was lifted out each time it was refilled with fresh charcoal. Two have the pot made into the oven, at the back. Two of the ovens are somewhat alike, with a door that opens on hinges; one door lifts up and the other drops down. Inside is a wire shelf on which rested an oblong pan.

The third tin oven is oblong and narrow and stands high on four thin legs of tin. This has two compartments with doors, each with two wire racks on which a pan rested. The doors are like those on footstoves, with wire hinges and a cotter pin for a latch. This long oven has a place for the pot of charcoal in the middle and over the hole was a sheet iron lid with a wire handle. That is missing in my stove. In the inside of the pot there is a hole which shows that a stove pipe was fitted into the chimney, carrying off the fumes of the burning charcoal.

Ever since I found these ovens, two up country and one in New Hampshire, I have called them biscuit ovens. Now, finding that crackers and biscuits are one and the same in early history and that charcoal was used for baking crackers, I have learned that the ovens were used to bake sea biscuits, ship biscuits, and even hard-tack. This was not for home consumption but to send off to the ships for the sailors.

* Crackers began to be manufactured in 1792 in New England by a Theodore Pearson who made thick, hard crackers in the seacoast town of Newburyport, Massachusetts. They were made with no yeast—only flour, water, and salt, in the same manner as of the early days. Half a century later, yeast was used, making a raised dough.

In Miltom, Massachusetts, in 1801, a man named Josiah Bent opened a bakery selling a water cracker. In Arlington, Massachusetts, Artemus Kennedy opened a bakery in 1805. Each bakery produced a lighter cracker with a smoother texture. Butter crackers were introduced and finally a sweet cooky. Thus began the house of the National Biscuit Company, coming into existence in 1898.

* From the Story of the National Biscuit Company.

9

WHEN CHARCOAL WAS MADE ON THE FARM

CHARCOAL MAKING WAS A VERY IMPORTANT INDUSTRY. MANY FARMS
made charcoal for their own use and for commercial purposes.

Sometimes a pit was dug and small logs of wood were stacked in an
upright position, making a tepee. Maple or birch was used, both hard
woods that made little ash. The logs could be laid cob-house fashion instead of in a tepee. Thick sod was laid on the structure, completely covering it. A vent was left at the top and one in the casing for a draft. The
fire was started by throwing a lighted brand down inside. As it burned,

Charcoal making on the farm

if the flame showed red, more wood was dropped in at the top and the side vent was closed.

Another way of laying the logs was in a ring, one layer piled upon another until the right quantity was laid. Sod and sand covered the logs and this method, too, called for vents, drafts, and constant watching.

It took three days and three nights to complete the process with constant watching. The worker took catnaps as he worked alone in the pasture. Then the sods were lifted off and the charcoal sticks taken away in barrels to a shed. There the pieces were separated from the powder. Splint baskets were used to sift out the powder; the baskets measured over two feet, with solid sides and openwork bottom. Another sifter was made of tin, round, with openwork bottom and a long wooden handle. Two such pieces are in my collection.

The powder was used in medicines, as a polish, and as fertilizer. The pieces were sold commercially to blacksmiths for their forge, to housewives for a quick fire and use in iron braziers and cracker ovens. Braziers were small round stoves that could be carried from room to room for the heat and to warm food on.

Charcoal making has been taken over by manufacturers, but one can still find charcoal rings out in pastures on some farms.

10

"AND ONE FOR THE POT"

SO THE OLD SAYING GOES AND IT IS DOLLARS TO DOUGHNUTS THAT AS each housewife starts her morning with the coffee pot in hand and measures the coffee, she says, "and one for the pot!"

What a difference a cup of good, hot coffee can make in a person's outlook for the day! Clear coffee, coffee with cream and sugar or with just cream—coffee is satisfying. Some people drink as many as five cups a day and some nationalities take more than others; but coffee starts the day.

Because the early Colonists had their cider, their rum, and their ale, they were not in need of other stimulating drinks. When whaling vessels began trading with foreign ports, coffee and tea were brought back along with sugar, molasses, and spices. It was then the table was supplied with far better things than home-grown products could produce.

The coffee bean was roasted before using, shaken over the fire. In my collection are coffee roasters, some more than a century old, used over the burning logs in the fireplace. The early roasters had long handles so that the worker might stand away from the heat. The holder was round or oblong, some smaller than others, closed air-tight. It was shaken over the fire like popcorn. The roaster for the old kitchen range had a short handle and a crank that moved the beans about as they roasted.

Records say that at first the beans were boiled whole and the water used as a drink. But the proper way was soon discovered and coffee mills put in their apperance, made of wood and brass with an iron crank, or made of all iron, screwed to the wall. Coffee as a drink did not become universal until the 19th century.

As for tea—what would the evening meal be without a cup of tea! Tea strong or tea weak, with lemon and sugar or with cream, it refreshes, relaxes, and stimulates the appetite. A variety of teas appear on the market today, coming from China principally, oolong and pekoe. The

And one for the pot

jasmine flower has been added to make a very delicate drink and now we have a spiced tea, flavored with spices and the ground rind of oranges and lemons. Remember the cambric tea when we were children? Because the grown-ups had their cup of tea, we had to have some and for us it was hot water with a little milk and sugar and sometimes a little, little bit of tea added. It is surprising to find that cambric tea is in the dictionary!

Can you imagine seeing tea leaves or coffee beans for the first time and wondering how to cook them! In the beginning, Colonists boiled the tea leaves, poured off the liquid and ate the leaves. In Old Salem, some of the families put butter and salt on the boiled leaves to make them more appetizing!

In England, tea was first sold in apothecaries, with a license. The English are known as great tea drinkers. America also consumed a great deal of tea until the Revolutionary War. When the cargo of tea arrived in Boston from England in 1773 and heavily taxed, it caused great resentment—"taxation without representation." With the scarcity of tea that followed the dumping of all the containers overboard, the Colonists turned to coffee. From then on, coffee has been more popular.

Tea has come into its own with afternoon tea parties. And in many establishments and libraries, mid-afternoon finds the workers sipping tea. In some large establishments, tea as well as coffee, is brought to the workers in containers. Many groups have rooms where they can brew their own tea.

We anticipate our coffee for the morning and we look forward to our tea in the afternoon or at the evening meal.

11

POTS AND PANS AND SUCH

WHILE I WAS HAVING A SESSION WITH THE EVENING'S DISHES, MY MIND suddenly was transferred to the pots and pans of long ago. I was scouring the aluminum pans with a cleanser and fine steel wool and wondered what it would be like to scour an iron kettle with no cleanser and no steel wool.

When I was very young, there were a few pieces of ironware in our kitchen. We had a big iron kettle for our weekly frying of doughnuts. Were those doughnuts good! And I just know that there are families today who still use such a kettle because nothing else will do for frying deep-fat doughnuts. It was somewhat shallow, that doughnut kettle, and if you went to auctions a few years ago, you would be sure to see such a. kettle come up for sale and take many bids.

We had an iron meat broiler. It was round, convex, with grooves running from the center down to the edge where there was a deep groove that caught the juices of the steak as it was broiling. This was placed over the open stove-hole and the steak was put onto it and turned until properly done.

We had an iron muffin pan, holding twelve oblong muffins. Some pans were round in shape. We used to have the most wonderful cornmeal muffins, with crispy browned crusts. Some pans of later date were made in the shape of an ear of corn, six or eight of them. I used our oblong holder for chocolate cakes and they are delicious, baked slowly in iron. You should see the way those old muffin pans sell at an auction and then you would know how superior they are to anything modern.

We had a round waffle iron that was used over the stove hole. The center part that held the mixture worked on a pivot so it could be turned over and each side of the waffle browned over the hot coals. Somehow, iron cooking utensils gave a wonderful crispness from a slow heat.

An old 17th-century rule for waffles reads: "I pound flour, quarter

pound butter, two eggs, beat, one glass wine and a nutmeg." Nutmegs
came whole and were grated on a small hand grater.

Mother tells me we had a gridiron, a flat round iron with a protruding handle. That was used when making griddle cakes, more properly
called pancakes. Grandma's old rule says: "Half a pint of milk, three
spoonsful of sugar, one or two eggs, a teaspoonful of dissolved saleratus
spiced with cinnamon or cloves, a little salt, and rose-water. Flour should
be stirred in till the spoon moves around with difficulty. Have the fat in
your skillet boiling hot, drop them in with a spoon, cook till thoroughly
brown." Those were cooked in deep fat. Ours were pan fried and called
flapjacks. But in Grandma's cookbook, the spelling is *flat-jacks,* because
they were flat instead of the ball dropped into deep fat. We had Indian
flapjacks made with Indian meal or cornmeal. We had buckwheat cakes
made with buckwheat flour, which according to Grandma's rule, had to
rise at night with yeast. It is fun to study the old cookbooks and little
wonder that there are many collectors who have them.

I barely remember our iron teakettle. It sat on the stove. The first
teakettles had three short legs to stand on the hearth. Later ones had an
extension that set into the stove hole and then came the flat ones on top of

Pots and pans and such

the stove. I can still recall the clink of the iron cover as it was lifted on its hinge when the kettle handle was pushed down to one side—an automatic arrangement. Heavy! It took muscle to handle the old iron pieces.

Those old iron pots must have been something to reckon with in cleaning. It is not possible to believe that the first scrubbing brush was a short splintered birch broom. In my notes I find there was a horsetail rush that was used for scouring. This had no leaves and a hollow stem and many of them were tied together. Home-made soap was used with water heated in an iron kettle. Scrubbing brushes came in due time. And for generations, home-made soap was used. Today's powders and scouring devices insistently remind us in advertisements and over the radio that we no longer need to struggle with pots and pans!

Those iron pots and pans gave way to tin and tin gave way to aluminum. The kitchen is changed from that drabness of a century ago to a gay display of shining tinware, while many are the copper pans that add to the cheerfulness of the workroom.

Perhaps today we are getting too soft. Too many electrical contrivances are not conducive to strong muscles.

12

OLD TIME COOKIES, CAKES AND DOUGHNUTS

WHAT WOULDN'T YOU GIVE TO BE TRANSPLANTED BACK TO THE OLD kitchens on baking day! This modern world of machines and buttons to press has lost all the romance the old days offered.

Remember the odors that came from the kitchen on Saturdays? The game that we used to play said that Monday was for washing, Tuesday was for ironing, Wednesday was for mending, Thursday was for calling, Friday was for cleaning, and Saturday was for baking. In the old days of baking in the brick ovens, baking was done in large quantities at one time; fifty pies, a dozen cornmeal puddings, a dozen or more bean porridges, loaves of brown bread, and loaves of wheat bread. It really was a baking day.

Fifty years ago, Saturday was still an important day. Cookies, cakes, and doughnuts took shape from the different kinds of dough. There was always a big cookie crock to fill, a cake box for the cakes, and a second crock for the doughnuts. Those crocks are prized by collectors today. Some of them were made by Norton and Company in Worcester, Massachusetts. There were sugar cookies, sprinkled with sugar, molasses cookies, and stuffed cookies that we called "monkey faces"—all plump, soft, and tasty. No fancy, dainty cookies the size of your thumb would do for a family of children. They were big and satisfying.

We children would always be on hand on baking day. The maid did not seem to mind as long as we kept busy and out of mischief. Three dollars and a half were top wages for a maid in those days and the servants were somehow a part of the family and shared our good times.

There were many cooky cutters but the one we liked the best was the man, with the dog coming next in choice. Those cooky cutters have gone into collections. The old ones had a scalloped edge, with the center design a bit lower in height so the pattern would not cut through the dough but merely make an imprint.

Old time cookies, cakes, and doughnuts

The ginger cooky man with currants for eyes and mouth and down the front for buttons was an exciting thing to make. We had to climb up onto a chair and rest our knees as we rolled and cut and stuck in the currants. One man and one dog would be our share of the morning's work. While we waited for the cooky to bake, we never lost sight of the bowl, waitng for the last bit to be taken out. Then "I choose the spoon! Let me lick the spoon!" Perhaps some dough stuck around the edges of the bowl and in would go our finger to get the last taste. We never helped with the monkey faces, but how we watched the maid cut the eyes and mouth on the top cover and then fill the bottom heaping with raisin mixture and then put the two pieces together. Those were licking good!

Cakes were always big and healthy looking, made with plenty of butter and left-over sour cream. The rules were those that had been passed down the generations; Grandma's sponge cake, Aunt Mary's sour milk cake, Aunt Lizzie's fruit cake—we have the rules still, written in fading ink in our old ragged cookbooks.

I can remember the old iron kettle for frying doughnuts. That went out as junk years ago, but those kettles are still being used for deep-fat frying. Our doughnuts were big, plump, and ragged, made with sour milk. What with pasteurized and homogenized milk today, there is seldom such a thing as sour milk. At the end of the frying came the doughnut balls for us children as we stood around watching and waiting. We still have the doughnut cutter, lying idle these many years and, in my collection, is a wooden cutter.

Another treat was the Sunday morning batch of fried doughnuts made from raised bread—"Rized bread" in the vernacular. Bread was always made on Saturdays and a batch was set aside for a Sunday morning break- fast of fried doughnuts and maple syrup. That was as much a part of Sundays as going to church and Sunday School and popping corn in the afternoon.

Odors are powerful things in bringing back memories. A bake shop throws out pungent odors today; we sniff as we pass and our minds go back to the Saturday mornings out in the big kitchen, kneeling on a chair, making ginger cookie men.

13

BAKED BEANS AND BROWN BREAD

Bean porridge hot,
Bean porridge cold,
Bean porridge in the pot, nine days old.

Some like it hot,
Some like it cold,
Some like it in the pot nine days old.

THAT JINGLE GOES BACK TO THE SETTLING OF MASSACHUSETTS IN 1620. In Colonial days, corn and beans were the staple fare. The corn was ground, mixed with water and made into cakes, and the beans were baked as porridge. Boston acquired the name of "Bean Town" because bean porridge was served daily for many years, either hot or cold.

The Bible tells of Esau selling his birthright for a mess of pottage, the early name for porridge. Porridge at that time was a liquid pudding, a cereal cooked with water and eaten in a soft condition.

A small flat bowl with an extending handle in which porridge was eaten was called a porringer. Later years saw them made of iron, pewter, and pottery as well as of wood.

The Indians baked their bean porridge in a fire hole, using receptacles they had made from clay in the soil. A hole was dug, two feet or more deep, lined with stones, with a stone at the bottom. A fire was made with maple or birch wood. When the stones were thoroughly heated, the embers were taken out and the pots of beans were put in to cook. A large flat stone was placed over the opening of the hole, making it heat tight. This cooking in the fire hole was the forerunner of the modern fireless methods.

In Colonial days, the beans were baked in the brick oven, the large oven at the side of the fireplace, called also the bake oven. The oven was first heated by burning wood with little ash, such as maple or birch. The embers were removed with an iron peel or shovel, called the ash peel. Next, the floor of the oven was swept with a splintered birch broom and the pots of beans placed inside. A wooden door cover was placed over the opening. The draft was inside the door, connected with the chimney. The wooden door cover was later replaced by one of tin and still later by one of iron, set on hinges with a sliding door for draft.

Baked beans and brown bread

The beans were first parboiled in water in an iron kettle hanging on the crane. When ready, they were prepared with generous pieces of salt pork and sweetening of maple sugar molasses. The pork came from the hogs that were slaughtered in the fall of the year and put into brine. The molasses came from a barrel of maple sugar, called maple molasses, trickling out the bunghole at the bottom. Cane sugar did not appear until later.

Many pots of beans were baked at one time, for the process of heating the oven and getting the beans ready for the long, slow cooking made a hard job for the housewife. Much cooking was done at one time, all on a Saturday. When the beans were done, the pots were taken out with a long wooden-handled tool with an iron half ring at the end. Sometimes the ring was a loop. Such a tool was necessary for drawing the pots and puddings from the deep oven. The pots were set away in the larder to freeze. When needed, a portion was brought out and put into the tin biscuit reflector oven, in front of the fire to heat, before serving.

Bean porridge and mush made up the daily fare for many years. Then the beans became a Saturday night meal, as regular as the rising and setting of the sun in the heavens.

Frozen porridge came into its own when the families went to market in the dead of winter. Several families joined in the trip, going in their own pungs. The sleighs were loaded with butter, cheese, pelts of sheep, hog bristles, hides of deer, dried peas and beans, homespun cloth, yarn, stockings and mittens, dried apples, and splintered birch brooms. These all came from the farm, produced by all hands of the family.

In exchange for these things, bartering was made for necessary commodities for the entire family, such as calico, boots, buttons, ribbons, trinkets, hats for men and bonnets for women, and many other things that could not be produced at home. The families took their dinner pails with them, holding bread, doughnuts, sausages, roast pork, cheese, and frozen porridge. A chunk of frozen porridge was always tied to the side of the sleigh, so when anyone felt the pangs of hunger, they would whack off a piece and eat it. The lunch was called mitchen.

In the course of time brown bread was made. There is a heavy pot of iron, tapering toward the bottom for brown bread, which was put into the brick oven. In my collection is one of tin with a hollow cylinder in the center, with a tight-fitting cover. The bread was taken out of the oven with the long pot hook.

A recipe in the family's cookbook of 1845 reads: "Take one quart of Indian meal, one quart of wheat meal, one quart of sour milk, half a teacupful of molasses, a heaping teaspoon of saleratus, and a little salt; stir it with a spoon, and bake it in a tin or iron basin, about two hours." The loaves of brown bread were filled with raisins, dried grapes from the vineyard.

Village shops sprang up in many towns, where the village baker baked the pots of beans and the loaves of brown bread. Here the families could bring their pots of beans Saturday morning and go after them Saturday afternoon, with a loaf of brown bread added. Often the pots were put in Saturday afternoon and were ready for Sunday breakfast. Sometimes, the baker went around gathering the pots of beans, returning them when done, with a loaf of bread. Many times young boys would take over the job for their families.

The old Wright's Tavern, Concord, Massachusetts, connected in history with the Revolutionary War, had a large fireplace and bake oven in the cellar. There the village baker held forth for many years, baking beans and brown bread in the deep oven. A tavern in another nearby town has a large fireplace and oven in the cellar as does one in Old Deerfield. It was in such fireplaces that whole animals were roasted on spits.

The old nursery rhyme is still alive today. And baked beans and brown bread are still a "must" for Saturday.

14

EARLY TABLEWARE AND EATING CUSTOMS

IT WAS NOT TOO LONG AGO THAT IT WAS THE COMMON THING TO HAVE a red table cloth on the diningroom table, or on the table out in the kitchen. Inverted tumblers, a glass spoon holder filled with spoons, a sugar bowl, napkins in a ring with the owner's name engraved on it, a tin bread tray shaped like a boat and filled with crackers—all of these were kept on the table from meal to meal and covered with a piece of cheese cloth. When it was time to set the table for breakfast, dinner, or supper, the cheese cloth was taken off and folded, ready to spread over the few pieces again after the meal was over and the dishes done.

Another memory of those days is of the round wire dish covers that were placed over the food. They came in sets of graded sizes. Flies were troublesome when there were barns and cattle.

Going back to the time of the Pilgrims, we read that they built houses of one room with a stone fireplace at the end and a loft overhead, reached by a ladder placed in a small opening. That one room served as living room, sleeping room, and dining room. Such small quarters necessitated furnishings that could be folded up or used for a double purpose. The bed could be turned up and the table taken apart and placed against the wall. The settle could be turned into a table.

The first table was a trestle table. The top was a wide plank, taken from the huge trees that measured many feet in diameter. The top rested on two standards held together by a long stretcher slipped through slots and pegged. After each meal, the stretcher was pulled out and the two standards and top stood up against the wall. Seats were benches and backless chair forms.

Another early table was the sawbuck table, the end supports made like a sawhorse. This, too, could be taken apart to make more space in that crowded room. The top was taken off the supports and stood up against the wall. A third type of table was the hutch table. The word

Early tableware

hutch means a chest or box, a container, such as a grain hutch or a rabbit hutch. The hutch table was made with a box-like base on legs and side arms. A large square or round top was hinged to the back of the arms. When tipped up, the table top became the back of a settle and when laid down it became a table on which the family ate.

Pewter was brought over on the various ships that came from across the water, in the form of pewter plates, salts, porringers, and spoons. But with heavy forests surrounding the few villages, it was a question of using the wood to rid the land of it. Houses, house furnishings, logs for heat and cooking, and tableware were made from wood for many generations.

The families of wealth continued to use pewter and china, but the village folk used woodenware; wooden bowls and porringers, plates, pitchers, and tankards. These were turned by hand on the early lathe and finished with a jackknife. Later, such articles as sugar bowls and spoon holders were made. Wooden spoons were used, made from pieces of wood with a jackknife.

The morning meal, breaking the fast of the night, was commonly mush, called also hasty pudding or Indian pudding. The Indians taught the white man how to cultivate the corn and prepare it for cooking. The mush was cooking slowly in the huge iron pots hanging over the fire through the night. Each one of the family served himself in his own bowl, eating it with syrup molasses or milk. Breakfast saw little ceremony. The drink in the early days was ale, until apple trees were sent over and planted, as early as 1634, when cider could be made. Water was not considered sanitary as a drink.

The noontime meal was dinner, when the family dined on a substantial meal. During the morning, roasts suspended on spits over the fire, to be served at dinner. Or in the iron pots, a mixture of meat and vegetables was cooking. This was called ragout or hotchpotch, the last name becoming our hodgepodge. Fingers and spoons were all that were necessary when eating, and jackknives were resorted to for cutting the meat. Quite often a guest would bring his own jackknife. And in his vest pocket he often carried a tiny tin grater, so that he might flavor his drink with nutmeg at the hearth.

When knives and forks appeared, they were first made with wooden handles and later with animal bone. The knife had a broad, curved blade and the early forks had two tines. It was the knife that conveyed the food to the mouth. The meat or fowl was held down with the fork in an upright position and the knife cut it and lifted it to the mouth. This manner of eating was general and was seen for more than one generation. Habits linger long.

Wooden plates were called trenchers. A commonly understood rule was that two people must eat from one trencher: man and wife or children. If a young man came to call and ate with his sweetheart, the family considered that to be an engagement.

A trencher in my collection measures 14 inches in diameter, coming from an old family in a nearby town. It is dated on the back in the old style ink and quill pen "1747 or earlier." Smaller plates average eight or nine inches in diameter to one of 5 inches for a child. Another trencher is as thin as a shell, 16 inches in diameter. That one has a story, as most of my pieces seem to have. One day, at an auction, this large trencher was put up for a bid. I could see that it had a crack where the rim joined the bowl part. And I could see that it had been mended. A dealer was pitted against me. He suddenly stopped. The auctioneer added a bird cage for more attraction but even then my bid was the only one to stand. I sold the bird cage for a quarter, on the spot. I saw how the trencher had been mended with a coarse piece of tow, laced through holes that had been bored with a tool. No telling how long that trencher had seen service, worn down to such a thinness. When I asked the dealer why he had stopped bidding, he said, "The darn thing was cracked!" A collector of woodenware thinks he is lucky if he owns something mended, for it shows thrift. A collector of glass, pottery, or china never wants an imperfect piece. In my collection are several pieces that have been mended with coarse tow.

The most unusual piece of workmanship is an oblong chopping tray.

The bottom evidently gave out from too much chopping, and it was cut with an even oblong hole. A piece of pierced tin was then tacked over the hole, very evenly. This then gave the housewife a strainer on the inside and a grater on the back side. After that, the ends of the bowl must have split, for there are strips of thin metal nailed across the ends to hold it together. Then it must have seen many more years of service. Such a piece has untold value to a collector.

A rare wooden platter was found at another auction. The owner called my attention to it and told me about it. It is oval, a yard long, with a five-inch rim. It was made to hold a stuffed pig—served head, tail, and feet, with an apple in its mouth. In the early fireplaces, ten or eleven feet long, such animals could be roasted whole. A long spit was thrust through the animal and this rested on andirons that had holders. The first spits were long wooden spears. Later ones were of iron with a sharp point at one end and a small curlicue at the other.

Salt bowls for the table were very important. The wooden ones measured as much as five inches in diameter. A salt bowl made a division line at the table, between the guests of high rank and those of low rank. It was in the same manner as that of today in seating a guest at the right of the host.

Salt was brought to the home in coarse form and crushed in the mortar and pestle. A portion was kept in the chimney cupboard over the fireplace to insure dryness. A toddy cup of wood was also kept in the cupboard, ready to be used when toddy was made in a tankard, heated with a toddy iron and served before the open fire. That small cupboard took the name of nightcap cupboard, for a last drink was often taken before retiring.

Sugar bowls were of various sizes, turned on the lathe by hand. They had a cover and some had a wire handle. These held the sugar from the maple tree, long before cane sugar was brought to the home. A lovely spoon holder of apple wood is in my collection, hollowed to a thinness, with a round bottom driven in. The pitcher of wood was called a noggin, shaped from one piece of wood, handle and all. The lathe was used to hollow the inside along with a chisel. Some are eight-sided and made in a set of three, graded in size. Other noggins are round and an odd one was made from a section of bamboo, with a wooden handle nailed onto it.

The one pitcher was passed from mouth to mouth at mealtime. Each member of the family seemed to have his own place from which to drink. A story goes that a guest drank from the wrong place and the small son cried out, "Don't drink there! That's Grandma's place!"

Going back to the days of the Romans, history relates that the men reclined on couches when they partook of a meal. The couch was set along one side of the long table. They were served from the opposite side. The painting of "The Last Supper" shows Christ and His disciples at one side only.

In the days of the Pilgrims, when the table was placed before the fire in winter, the family sat at one side, facing the fire, for heat and light. Serving from the kettles hanging on the crane was simplified when one side of the table was open. This custom of sitting on one side soon changed and the families sat around the table.

Wooden table ware was used well into the 19th century. Pewter and china was used in the homes of the wealthy. After 1800, woodenware gradually disappeared and china and glass was found in all the homes.

The dining room became a place of beauty with fine furniture made by master craftsmen. China, glass, and silver were arrayed on fine damask linen. However, the red tablecloth was used for many generations in country towns. And woodenware is found now only in museums.

15

BOWLS TODAY AND YESTERDAY

UP IN VERMONT, HIGH UP IN THE MOUNTAINS, IS THE SMALL VILLAGE
of Weston. The village has a widely known Country Store, a grist mill, a
famous old tavern, and, for summer visitors, a playhouse and the inevit-
able antique shop. There, too, is a bowl mill where they turn out bowls
for trade.

Around the corner from the Country Store and the small Village Post
Office it stands, a gray, unpainted shed. Out in the side yard is a pile
of unfinished bowls in block form, imperfect and marked 25 cents each.
From the large open door comes the clean smell of shavings and sawdust.

Stepping into the mill, we saw a man at the lathe, turning out bowls
from a block of wood, measuring 15 inches. There were four different
sizes of arms or blades, each with a curved head, which made four different sizes of bowls. The block was held in a revolving vise and the first,
the smallest, arm or blade was set into a holder.

As the block of wood turned around the blade, which was steadied by
the worker, a hollow center was cut into the block. This was for the smallest bowl. The second largest blade was used in the same manner, cutting
out a bowl, making a thickness of three-quarters of an inch. A third and
fourth blade was used in turn, making four bowls from one block of wood,
of the same thickness but graded in size. A pile of fragrant shavings was
on the floor and a big wooden box nearby was full—ours for the taking.

Another man polished and stained the bowls. A counter at the front
of the mill by the door was full of finished bowls, ready for retail trade
or for orders.

In an adjoining shed was a long trunk of a tree lying ready to be
used. We asked what kinds of wood were used for those modern bowls
and the answer was maple, beech, and ash, all hard wood. The tree had
to be at least 24 inches in diameter.

Another product of the bowl mill is the Lazy Susan. That dates back into antiquity and is called a "table center" in the old country. Two flat plates, each with a raised edge and one being less in diameter than the other, are fastened together by a center pivot. The large plate is on a low standard and the smaller one is placed a few inches above that. They both pivot separately.

The Lazy Susan was used in the center of the table, generally round, acting as two smaller tables on top of the regular table. On each of the revolving tables, plates of food, seasoning, and condiments were placed. Whenever a member of the family wanted something, he or she turned one or the other small table and helped themselves. This Lazy Susan was often made as one wooden plate revolving on the main table.

A common accessory of 50 years ago was a revolving silver holder, containing four or five glass castors, each one filled with a condiment; salt, pepper, vinegar, and mustard. They were very ornamental with a silver holder of elaborate pattern and castors of thin etched glass. Sometimes a silver bell hung from the top of the handle. Common usage has given the word "caster" to the holder itself, but Webster says that the *set* of glass bottles was called a caster.

A bowl was doubtless one of the first eating requisites. Savages and the Indians used a hollow stone. But the Indians knew trees and they made bowls from the wood. The most beautiful of all the bowls left to posterity are those made from the burl or wart of the tree. The Indians called this a knot. It was a diseased growth coming on the trunk and the round shape suggested a bowl. Those on the ash and maple were the toughest; the other were punky. The growth measured three and four feet in diameter on those first huge trees in the virgin forests.

The Indian cut off the wart and stripped it of its bark. His tools were of stone, bone, shell, and flint. To hollow the flat side, he first charred the wood by burning bits of bark on it. As the wood became soft, he began to cut. He burned and cut, a long tedious job. The bowl was more oval than round and was cut to a thinness. The tool marks can generally be seen on the early Indian bowls. One in my collection is said to have been made by an Indian named Huge Pie in the year 1803. It has handle holes and the tool marks are very pronounced. The Indians generally made handle holes or extending lips by which to carry the bowl. His wooden bowls were used primarily as containers for food, whereas hollowed stones were used as grinding vessels.

Continuing to describe the Indian's work with trees, it is interesting to know how his dugouts or canoes were made. He selected his tree, peeled off the bark and shaped it, making pointed ends. Then he cut the inside, making it of a necessary thinness for the weight when finished. The dugout or canoe had to be wider at the center. To do this, he filled it with water and dropped in a stone that had been heating in the fire for some time. He then wedged a stick from side to side. The water warmed by the stone expanded the sides. Each day, he put in a heated stone and wedged in a longer stick until the canoe was of the necessary width, for balance and swiftness.

To return to the bowls, those taken from a wart or knot made a beautiful mottled and streaked grain in the finished wood. The irregular grain made tough wood. There is such a bowl in my collection, round and measuring nearly two feet in diameter. It shows the grain of the tree in circular lines and in perpendicular lines. Some of these bowls measured four feet long and three feet wide. I also have a burl as it was cut from the tree and peeled of its bark.

Another beautiful wood was the bird's eye maple. That, too, was a diseased growth of the grain, which left small eyes in the disrupted rings. It was made into very attractive bowls. Plain maple, chestnut, and oak were other woods that were used. A student of wood and trees finds much of interest in bowls.

Bowls of yesterday and today

There were bowls of every size and for all purposes; the small ones for salt, those for eating, and the larger ones for holding stews and for performing many tasks in the kitchen. When a collector of woodenware sees the various bowls, he understands the purpose for which they were made.

One of my first bowls was long and narrow, the width of the chopping knife. It was used as a chopping bowl, for the marks of the knife are there. Great quantities of meat went under the chopping knife, to be used in stews. Pork for sausages was chopped, too, for there were no grinders in those early years. To see an array of 70 chopping knives such as are in my collection, all different and hand-made, makes one realize the creative ability of the blacksmith, who designed them and forged them on his anvil.

My next bowl came from a carpenter who had dismantled the Shaker Colony at Enfield, New Hampshire. It is painted green on the outside and has two large copper handles fastened to the rim. This was a serving bowl of the Shakers. Many bowls show for what purpose they were made. One is stained dark showing that it held grease after the fat was tried out. Another one is bleached, showing it was used either to hold lye that was used in making soap or for a batch of bread. Both of these bowls were made from the burl.

A rare lignum vitae bowl came from an Antique Shop on Martha's Vineyard. Lignum vitae, the heaviest wood known, comes from the West Indies. The bowl is shaped like an oblong soup tureen with two lip handles. The inside is worn down from the chopping knife. It was in the beginning of my collecting that I found the bowl. I was sitting on an old broken-down sofa in the shop, showing the dealer pictures of my woodenware. He abruptly got up and went into the back part of the house and returned with the bowl under his arm. "This was my grandfather's, made on a whaling vessel leaving New Bedford. I want you to see it. But I am not selling it." Imagine how I longed to own such a bowl! We talked of many things in the shop, but all the time I was thinking of the bowl. I even made him a price. I again told him of my collection and of the need for preserving those old pieces that might be sold and scattered to the four winds. He made no comment. I turned to go. I again made him my offer, probably with a stronger plea that the bowl should be in my home. He followed me to the car with the bowl under his arm. Then with tears in his eyes, he said, "You may have it for your collection." The transaction was quickly made. The bowl stands on the top of a low cabinet, inviting everyone to inspect it. It is lignum vitae. There is a burnt spot on one side where it was left too close to the fire and the inside shows mute evidence of the length of service it saw on board a whaling vessel.

There were many sizes of eating bowls, from a soup bowl ten inches in diameter to a child's bowl of four inches. With a wooden bowl and a wooden spoon, each member of the family ate his mush and milk and his stews. When I was a child, I was told a story of an old grandpa who ate from a wooden bowl with a wooden spoon, sitting by the stove in the kitchen. A little grandchild was talking to him one day and said, "Grandpa, when I am old, will I have to sit by the stove and eat from a wooden bowl?" After that, Grandpa ate at the table with the family.

Many a bowl served as a wash basin out on a bench at the back door. Quite often, the basins were by the pump in the kitchen, the water dished out with a dipper made from a gourd. And one oval-shaped bowl in my collection held salt on the table, bleached white except for the upper part where the salt did not reach. The owner told me it had been used in a barn to hold salt for the cattle, but that was not reasonable, for the force of the cow's tongue would have pushed over the bowl.

In the homes of the well-to-do families, salt was put onto the table in large gold, silver, or pewter holders or salt-cellars. In the homes of those of lesser wealth, salt bowls were made of wood. The largest one in my collection measures seven inches in diameter, while the smallest, as individual salts, measures about two inches.

The story of salt goes back to earliest times. Roman soldiers were given part payment in salt, which brought about the expression, "He is not worth his salt." The Arabs' expression of friendship was to say, "There is salt between us." I wonder why we throw salt over our left shoulder whenever we spill any, to avoid a quarrel!

Drinking bowls of wood were found in the old countries across the water, but seldom in this country. I have a small wooden mug. The family drank from one pitcher, passed from mouth to mouth, while in the homes of the wealthy, there were those of pewter, silver, and glass, classified as goblets.

One huge bowl which I could not buy was made of light-weight wood such as poplar or apple wood. It measures at least three feet in diameter. It was used to dry fruit out in the sun or possibly beans before they were shucked. A similar light-weight bowl of smaller size is in my collection, coming from Pennsylvania and used for drying fruit or beans. It is almost flat with two handle lips.

The Indian made his bowls by hand with his primitive tools. But the white man fashioned his on a lathe. The first lathe for turning out wooden objects was conceived in Holland in 1295. This worked only half circle, run by a pole overhead, suspended from the ceiling. It was called a spring pole lathe because the pole sprung back when released after making each half turn. The next lathe was called a mandrel lathe that turned full circle.

Today's round bowls turned out by machinery for trade, up in Weston, and in other sections of New England, are highly polished. They are not thin or as carefully made as those of a century or more ago. Their uses are limited to salads, popcorn, rolls, and muffins; and often as a holder for gourds in the fall of the year. This revival of the custom of using wooden bowls and other woodenware brings a bit of the past in today's ways of living.

16

POP CORN AND MILK EVERY SUNDAY NIGHT

REPOSING IN MY COLLECTION IS A LITTLE CORN POPPER. YOU HAVE TO use your imagination to know what it is, because of its construction. You have to think back 100 years when the little popper with a few kernels of corn in it was held over the open fire on the hearth. It is tiny, square, made of sheet iron with a wire mesh bottom. That wire was the clue for its use. It would have held one quart of popped corn. It has a long wooden handle that is scorched from having been held too close to the heat.

Popped corn must have been the white man's discovery. Governor Withrop of Boston wrote in his diary in 1630 that when corn was "parched" it turned inside out and was "white and floury." We can imagine the happy group sitting in front of the hearth, watching with

Popped corn and milk every Sunday night

expectancy for the corn to pop. A big wooden bowl stood ready on the table to hold it. In those days of scarcity, when small portions were a common thing, a quart of popped corn was considered plenty. It was eaten with great relish.

There are many of us who remember the Sunday night bowl of popped corn and milk. It was only on that one night of the week that we had it and did we look forward to it! We liked best to pop it in an iron spider with butter, on the stove top. The kernels were put in with a generous piece of butter and a cover was placed on. Gently shaking the spider back and forth soon made the kernels burst open. We poured the "white and floury" kernels into an earthen bowl, salted them, and sat down to our feast of corn and milk. Corn in the early days had black or dark red kernels; golden and yellow corn was a later product.

A wire popper came onto the market. Melted butter was poured over the corn after it was put into a bowl. It was never as tasty as what was popped in the spider. One day at an auction, I bought several corn poppers that were put up as a lot. The only one I wanted was made of sheet iron. I gave away the wire ones on the spot—for a quarter if I remember correctly. The iron popper was round and shallow. The wire cover lifted on a hinge and the short handle showed that it was meant to be used on the stove top. You could put butter into it as you shook the kernels back and forth, slowly at first and then faster and faster. I revelled in my purchase and used it every Sunday night for many years.

Where are the corn balls that we used to make on festive occasions? After we had boiled our molasses to a certain consistency, watching it spin a thread on the end of the spoon, we dropped in a piece of butter. Then we stirred in the popped corn, only the largest kernels. We would wet our hands in cold water and then shape the corn into balls, large, small or medium, pressing them together hard. When cold, the balls were wrapped in wax paper, or left on a platter to be eaten. At Christmas time, we would first wrap the balls in wax paper and then tie them up in red tissue paper. How the family loved to bite into our popped corn balls! We often made them for church fairs or other similar places.

Popped corn has ceased to be special. Today, it can be found on every street corner, buttered or mixed with cheese or molasses, or chopped and made into flat cakes. It has lost its romance. We rarely see the old-fashioned corn balls.

Changes often make for satiation.

17

OUR ANCESTORS HAD FROZEN FOOD

DEEP FREEZE UNITS HAVE BECOME SO POPULAR NOW THEY ARE NO longer a novelty. Families are adding them to their other equipment and many towns have lockers which can be rented. Refrigerators are being made with an inner compartment where food can be frozen and there is a large refrigerator with shelves which holds nothing but frozen food. But the idea of freezing is not a new invention.

In 1950, an Associated Press report from San Diego, California, told of pies flown across the country. The process of freezing was developed during World War II and this particular bakery was turning out 15,000 pies daily from its freezing plant. Those frozen pies were sent by refrigerator cars as well as by airplane.

A new idea? "There's nothing new under the sun." Such a thing as frozen food can be traced to prehistoric times and followed down the ages. Our ancestors in these shores knew of no other way of preserving food for the winter months than by freezing it. Every family had a larder or pantry and in that large room food was stored to freeze.

Pies were baked in the deep bake oven at the side of the fireplace, *shoved* in and taken out with a wooden pie peel or *shovel*. In my museum is an odd peel that shows signs of having been used to put pies into the bake oven. It is half a pair of bellows. It has the shaped handle, the slightly hollowed round head, and the edge is filled with nail holes where the leather was once tacked on. I often wonder if the other half is doing duty elsewhere.

Apple pie, made of dried slices of apple, was the favorite, but pies filled with wild berries and fruits and pumpkins and mincemeat were made in every kitchen. Taken from the oven, they were carried into the larder to freeze and to be kept until needed. Wire pie racks have not entirely disappeared today; these held many pies, one above the other to the number of fifty.

When a pie was wanted for dinner, it was taken out of the cold room and placed in a tin reflector oven before the fire, to thaw out before it was served. Crockery plates were replaced by those of tin, which were large and deep with a fluted rim.

Another popular dish baked on Saturdays in the deep oven was Indian pudding. It was no small sized pudding dish; it was one with a generous diameter. In the small town of Paxton, north of Worcester, where I spent my childhood summers, there is a crossroad about a mile out of town. It has been called Puddin' Corner. This name clung to it after some housewife once living there made an Indian pudding in a large and deep tin milk pan, for a church sociable. In my collection is a round wooden box that was used to carry two pies to a sociable. Someone conceived the idea of putting a round rack on two short legs, so that one pie could be on the bottom of the box and the other on the rack. Those Indian puddings were set away with the pies to freeze.

Baked beans with molasses or maple sugar and plenty of pork from the family pig were baked, many pots at a time and put away to freeze. These were brought out as needed and warmed before the fire or in later years, in the oven of the kitchen range. No one can forget the game and

Our ancestors had frozen food

rhyme: "Bean porridge hot, bean porridge cold." We used to play the game with our hands, slapping our own and the other player's hands alternately as we sang our rhyme.

A favorite way of using frozen porridge was to take a chunk and tie it to the side of the sleigh seat when the family went to market in the dead of winter. If anyone was hungry, they broke off a piece and ate it.

Ham was first smoked in the smoke oven and then packed away in oats or charcoal in a bin stored in the larder. Sometimes a whole pig was smoked and packed away to be served in slabs and slices; meat, strips of bacon, and slabs of pork. Once I went to an old house in New Hampshire to see a new acquaintance. I was taken all over the house and outside. In what was a small barn was a contraption for scalding hogs. An eight-inch pole ran from loft to loft in front of the doorway. One end was thrust through the hub of a large wheel. A horseshoe was driven into the pole about midway into which a rope was swung. The hogshead of scalding water was placed beneath the rope. After the hog was killed it was swung up and dropped into the hogshead, the pole taking the weight of the animal and turned by the big wheel. This loosened the bristles. It was one more original creation thought out by an early settler for doing a hard job in as easy a way as possible. It was called a *hog reel* and turned by a windlass.

In the larder, hanging from the ceiling, was a Dutch apron. This was made with a circular band of iron, a foot in diameter, from which small rods extended a foot or more to a center ring. The ring was fastened to a hook and pulley in the ceiling and the crown could be raised or lowered by a rope through the pulley. Around the band of the crown were eight or nine hooks. On these were hung fish and meat that had been prepared for winter freezing, the fish hanging by their gills and the meat stabbed onto the hooks.

With the long winter months in the northern sections, it became a necessity to store food by freezing. Only once in the winter did the families go to market and every family knew the need of freezing and storing food. Families were large and provisions were ample, coming from the farm.

The idea of frozen foods is not new.

18

BACK TO THE INDIANS' FIRELESS COOKER

WE READ NOW THAT THE CAMPFIRE GIRLS ARE COOKING IN A HOLE-IN-the-ground. It is called Imu, taken from the methods of cooking in Hawaii. The account from Ida Bailey Allen says it is similar to the casserole of France.

Looking away from Hawaii and France, we have learned how the Indians of North America cooked in their hole-in-the-ground. They dug a deep hole and lined it with thin stones. Then they built a fire of maple or beech wood on the floor. When the stones were throughly heated the embers were taken out. The pot of food or part of a whole animal to be cooked was laid inside. The hole was sealed airtight with animal skins and boughs. This cooking took many hours. It was the forerunner of the fireless cooker of today. The Indians called it a fire hole.

I can tell of an unusual fireless cooker in my own house, some 60 years ago. Mother had no Indian blood in her, but she conceived her own method of making a cooker. She took the big papier mâché washtub that had wire handles with a wooden grip. (I wonder whatever became of that!) She had it brought up from the cellar. Along with it came two bricks. She heated the bricks in the stove oven. When they were as hot as could be, Mother put them in the bottom of the tub. A whole ham had been cooking in a kettle on the stove top. The kettle was sealed airtight, and in it went, on top of the bricks.

Then Mother packed the tub with old blankets. Over all, she put an old shawl. It was her grandmother's shawl and it had come to a lowly end of service. (It finally went into a braided rug.) I can see the big tub enveloped with the shawl over in the kitchen corner, making a picture which I can call forth today. The ham was cooked perfectly and most tender and Mother was proud of her feat.

It wasn't many years before fireless cookers appeared on the market. I recall they held soapstone plates that had to be heated to produce the

Back to the Indians' fireless cooker

means of cooking. It was a low box-like structure of wood and tin and it had two cells with air-tight covers. The rules for operating them came with the outfit.

We have a single-container, fireless cooker that has an electric unit. That must be 40 years old. We plug it into an outlet in the wall. We can bake beans, a chicken with pared potatoes inside it, and meatloaves. It is perfect for baking apples and pears. Our baked beans are lima beans with pork and brown sugar and salt. They are done like regular baked beans except for the brown sugar taking the place of molasses. I make brown bread and bake the mixture in three old baking powder cans, putting the cans on a rack in the fireless. They go with the beans and make a wonderful Saturday night supper.

Today, electric stoves have a deep well which carries out the same principle as the Indians' fire hole or the hole-in-the-ground. It is such a simple thing to prepare a dinner, put it into the well, turn on the current, and leave the rest for the heat. It takes a few hours but nothing as compared to the hours of labor put in by the Indians' fire hole.

19

BROOMS AND BRUSHES

EVERY SPRING WHEN HOUSECLEANING LOOMS, THE HOUSEWIFE LOOKS over her brooms, brushes, and mops. There are so many of these cleaning aids today, work is made as easy and as simple as possible.

Not so in the times of past generations. Brooms were not numerous even though they could be had for the making. The word broom was the name of the species of coarse shrubs whose small branches were tied together to make a brush for sweeping. Another name for the shrub was *besom,* which is the word for "broom" used in the Bible. Isaiah says, "I will sweep with the besom of destruction." Those twigs were fastened together as a brush, either by themselves or to a handle. Such a broom or brush was used to sweep the hearth and the kitchen floor. Today, there are such brooms made of twigs tied together.

A more sturdy broom and one that did better work was the one made from a birch sapling and called a splinter birch broom. A slender white birch sapling, or sometimes a blue beech, was cut the proper length for a broom and peeled of its bark. The end was splintered at the end of the handle and tied. Then the core was taken out to make it less bulky. A foot up on the handle, above the first splinters, the wood was splintered and turned over the first set. The whole was tied with a second cord. Then the handle was pared to the right size and smoothed. The cutting was done when the wood was wet.

The Indian taught the white man how to make those splintered birch brooms and even young boys became skillful with a jackknife. Making a broom took about two evenings. Then the boys would trudge to the nearest town with the brooms on their backs and sell them for six cents each. Girls, too, made brooms and they bought ribbons for their hair.

Such a broom was made in a shorter size for scrubbing the iron pots and pans. It was called a brush then and was also used to sweep out the

Brooms and brushes

floor of the bake oven after the embers had been taken out, making it
ready for baking bread.

One day when giving a lecture, I was telling of my brush broom as
I held it in my hands. Someone in the back seat rose and said she had
seen tiny ones used for beating eggs and whipping cream. That was called
a *whisk*. Again, at one of my lectures in Boston, a little, genteel lady was
sitting in the front seat holding a small package wrapped in tissue paper.
After my talk, she took off the wrapping and showed me a tiny whisk.

It had been used by her ancestors down South and it was the only bit of her old home that was left. She would not part with it, prizing it as an heirloom.

The climax of all of that was when I found such a small whisk at an auction. That in itself is a story. Now, in my collection, I have a long floor broom, several shorter scrubbing brooms, and a tiny whisk. The whisk does not have a cord tied around the splinters, but instead, some of the last splinters were braided into a tiny braid and that was used to tie the whole together.

One more brush was a turkey wing. That, too, is in my collection. A turkey wing was stiff, broad, and heavy at one end, tapering at the tip of the feathers. The broad end was bound with a piece of cloth, black calico, as a handle.

Sand was used on the old kitchen floors, as sawdust is used today. Doubtless, this would be swept up occasionally and new sand put on. In taking down old houses, sand is often found, having sifted between the cracks of the wide floor boards.

Grown in the fields of North America was found a wild shrub known as a variety of sorghum. It grew to a height of eight or ten feet. This was used especially for brooms. A machine was invented that held a wooden handle onto which was fastened a number of stalks. These were woven into shape to make a flat, curved-top broom. Then the stalks were tied and the ends cut the proper length. This broom corn grew commonly in sections along the Connecticut River. Such machines have been preserved in Museums.

20

BASKETS HAVE ALWAYS BEEN USEFUL

ONE DAY AT AN AUCTION, I BOUGHT A GOOSE BASKET, MADE OF SPLINT. As I was leaving the grounds, I passed a man going back to the tent. "What'cher got there?" he asked.

"A goose basket; a basket to keep the feathers in," I said.

"Where ya goin' to get'cher feathers?" he asked next.

"I guess you don't know too much about these old things," I said.

"No," came the reply. "I buy furniture."

That goose basket made of splint is shaped like a big round demijohn, two feet high and two feet at the bulge. It has an opening about eight inches across. There is a large and taller goose basket in my collection shaped like a big bottle with a cover. Having such a basket, I learned how it was used.

Geese were plucked for their down three or four times a year. A stocking was pulled over their heads to keep them from biting. Sometimes the head was held between the knees. Or if the housewife owned a splint basket, the head of the bird was thrust into the opening and with one hand holding the legs of the bird, the worker plucked the bird with the other hand. The feathers dropped down into the basket and remained there until they were used in mattresses.

There were three grades of beds; one had a mattress filled with down for a guest, one had a mattress filled with common feathers for the husband and wife and a third made of oak leaves, corn husks, or cat-tail leaves for transient peddlers. The leaves and husks were shredded with a hetchel. A down pillow has always been an important part of bed furnishings.

In the bedroom of Clara Barton's birthplace in Oxford, Massachusetts, is a big square splint basket, with a cover. It is at least a yard square and two feet high. It was used for the feather bed in the summertime. When cold weather came, back onto the bed it went. In Fruitlands, a

Museum in Harvard, Massachusetts, the home of Bronson Alcott, another kind of basket held the feather bed. It is round, a scant three feet in diameter and two feet high, with a heavy cover. This is made of reed.

I have recently found a splint feather bed basket. It is round, a yard in diameter, with a round deep cover. The depth of the cover was the clue that it was for a feather bed. The dealer had no knowledge of it. It is rare.

Trees used for making splint were cut in May, while the sap was running. Either an ash tree or a hickory tree was taken for splint. It was hauled into the yard, split into four sections; and left to dry. Then it was stripped of its bark. With a heavy wooden mallet, the sections were pounded to loosen the wood. With a sharp draw knife, a strip of wood was started and pulled down the entire length. After all the wood had been stripped, some pieces wide and some narrow, the strips were put into a brook and weighted down. There they remained until they were to be used for the various baskets. The strips were shaved thin on a shave horse, some wide and some narrow.

The Indians knew the art of making splint and they made many baskets; basketry and bead work seem to be associated with the Indians. They often painted their baskets, taking the juice of berries and applying it with a quill or feather. The flower designs were small, put on each square of the weaving.

One of the most necessary articles in the home was a cheese basket. Every family had cows and every family made butter and cheese. Cream was kept in a tub as it collected day by day. To prepare it for cheese, rennet was poured in to coagulate it. Rennet was made from the stomach of a young calf that had had nothing but milk. This stomach was washed and turned and washed a second time. It was then cut into pieces and put to soak in water until the time came for using it to coagulate the cream. The mixture was then called curds. It was put into a piece of cheese cloth and placed in a splint basket, a cheese basket, on a rack over a tub. We all remember the story of Miss Muffet eating her curds and whey. The pigs had the liquid, the whey. Drained, the curds were made into various kinds of cheese.

The cheese basket was made of inch-wide strips, started by crossing strands to make hexagonal openings for draining. When the sides were turned up, the basket became round in shape. A double binding of splint was wound around the edge. The baskets measure two or three feet in diameter. Today, these baskets are used as magazine holders or for the family cat or dog.

My largest basket of splint is an apple-drying basket. It measures four feet by two feet and is shallow. A handle of wound splint runs from

Baskets were always useful

side to side across the middle. The splint is wide and the strands were woven with openings at the bottom but with solid sides. The basket bottom is stained dark from the juice of the apples. A collector of woodenware likes to see stains and marks, which show how tools and implements were used.

A friend in New Hampshire found the basket and sold it to me. He then wanted me to go with him and see the man who made it. I followed in my car for several miles through country roads until we came to a beautiful old white house. The man heard us coming and was out on the lawn. He did not invite us into the house and I suspected it was because he lived alone and his housekeeping would not bear inspection. He told us he made his long basket for drying sliced apples. The apples were pared and cored and then sliced into rings. He said it took a bushel of apples to make seven pounds of dried apples. Half the basket was filled with slices and that end was placed out the window, resting on the sill. The other half was filled and the basket was rotated until all the slices had been dried.

Slices of apples were also dried on slatted racks hanging from hooks in the ceiling over the fire. This is the function of the hooks found in the ceilings of the old kitchens. A second way of cutting apples to dry them was to pare them and quarter them. The quarters were strung on strings and thrown over racks not unlike those used for clothes.

The old man illustrated his lesson by cutting an apple with his jackknife. He pared it, cored it, sliced it, and quartered it. He ate the pieces as he worked, his little beard pumping up and down as he ate and talked. It made a very realistic picture of how the splint apple drying basket was used. When we returned to my friend's house and I headed for home, my friend asked me if I remembered how many pounds of dried apples came from a bushel of raw apples. I could answer promptly. Seven pounds.

Other rare pieces of splint in my museum are two pairs of ox muzzles, a vinegar funnel and an eel trap. Before wire was made, splint was used for many things. The ox wore a muzzle to prevent it from eating as it worked. Some muzzles are solid like a basket of narrow splint, shaped long and narrow, while others were made with openings. In this, four heavy rods of hickory run from the center to the rim to support the splint and keep it from breaking. The muzzles were tied around the horns with a cord. Both types of muzzles are in my collection.

A vinegar funnel was used to transfer vinegar from the big barrel to small kegs. It is eighteen inches long with an opening of thirteen inches and is a rare example of handwork with both wide and narrow strips of splint.

The eel trap is another beautiful piece of handwork, measuring two feet in length. It is cylindrical in shape and inside is a conical set of fine strips of splint that end part way down in a narrow point. When the eel went in, he could not get back. A cloth bag was fastened to the end into which the eel crawled and was captured.

Splint baskets of all descriptions are found, from an egg basket to the one used for the washing that went onto the hemp line out in the yard. The Shakers made many baskets, often in sets or nests. In Fruitlands is a tall round basket that was used in drying the hops. Hops were commonly grown and used for both medicinal purposes and in brewing drinks. The lees of hop water were used in making yeast. In Still River, a part of Harvard and nearby to Fruitlands, is another large basket. This was filled with hops every season and carried into the attic of the lean-to. When the house was enlarged and the lean-to made into rooms with an attic included, the basket remained where it was. It is still there—it cannot be taken down the stairs and it cannot go out the small attic window. So it remains, a mute reminder of those old days of hop picking.

Many families made their own charcoal, burning birch or maple wood. In my collection is a charcoal sieve with which the charcoal was sifted. It measures about two feet square and is shallow. The bottom is like a sieve and the sides are solid. The powder was used in medicine and as a fertilizer. The pieces were used in small stoves, cracker ovens, and by the blacksmith. Charcoal gave out twice as much heat as other fuels.

Chairs were seated with splint. It is recorded that splint was used before rush because so much wood was at hand. The Shakers not only made baskets but they seated chairs. Splint found in old chairs has lasted 200 and more years. The old splint was air-dried; today's splint is kiln-dried and much inferior in quality.

Splint baskets recall the old days when everything was made from the trees at hand and made by the various members of the family.

21

MARROW BONES AND MARROW SCOOPS

HAVE YOU EVER STOPPED TO WATCH A DOG HOLD A BONE IN HIS FRONT paws and crack it for the meat that is inside? That meat is the marrow and every dog knows that it is a choice morsel. All animals are given strong teeth so they might crack bones for the marrow inside.

One day, in my piece of beef shank, there was a bone an inch and a half in diameter. When the shank with the bone was cooked, the marrow came out, a string of meat at least three-quarters of an inch in diameter. If was my first beef stew in the making and it was the first time I had encountered a piece of cooked marrow.

Among my notes, I found that in the time of Queen Anne of England, at the end of the 17th century and the beginning of the 18th, it was the height of fashion to serve bones at the table for the marrow that was in them. The marrow, being fatty, has a distinct flavor.

Slender silver marrow scoops, tools eight and nine inches long, were made with a short, narrow scoop at the end, which could be inserted into the bone to draw out the marrow. These silver tools were laid by the plate along with other silver used in eating. A few such silver scoops are found in museums. The one I have is steel, probably used by families of humble means.

In an old cookbook of 1822, called *The Cook's Oracle,* a rule is given concerning marrow bones: "Saw the bones even, so they will stand steady; put a piece of paste into the ends; set them upright in a sauce pan and boil until done enough; a beef marrow bone will require from an hour and a half to two hours, according to the thickness of the bone. Serve fresh toasted bread with them." One cannot but wonder why the bone did not tip over when a silver scoop was thrust into it, and why the bone did not soil the fingers which held it.

Another rule of a different sort is found in the *Complete Housewife* or *Accomplish'd Gentlewoman's Companion.* "To make marrow pastries:

A dog and his bone

Make your little pastries the length of a finger, and as broad as two fingers, put in a large piece of marrow dipt in egg, and season'd with sugar, cloves, mace and nutmeg; strew them with a few currants on the marrow, bake or fry them."

Serving the prepared bones went out of fashion, for later cookbooks do not mention them. The marrow was taken out of the bone and served in stew along with the other meat. The first mention of stew is in the Bible, Esau's mess of pottage. Then we find the Colonists called their meat stews such name as ragout and hotchpotch.

We can understand after seeing narrow scoops why dogs struggle to crack a bone to find the bit of meat inside. And we can also understand the expression "chilled to the bone" and "Chilled to the very marrow."

22

HOT CROSS BUNS ON GOOD FRIDAY

Hot cross buns, hot cross buns,
One a penny,
Two a penny,
Hot cross buns!
Who'll buy my buns, who'll buy my buns,
One a penny,
Two a penny,
Hot cross buns!

IT WAS MANY GENERATIONS AGO THAT SUCH A CRY CAME FROM THE streets of more than one town in England, from vendors selling buns on Good Friday. Two celebrated bun houses in Chelsea, England, long since gone, sold hot cross buns from morning until night. Hundreds of eager buyers bought them.

The word *bun* has its origin in Scandinavia, but the old English word "buyne" means "a swelling" and that may be the source of the English bun.

It was an ancient rite of the Saxons to eat cakes in honor of the Goddess of Spring. They were consecrated cakes called Simnell, made of fine flour and water. For many years in the early centuries, there was a Sunday in mid-Lent called Mothering Sunday, when children were admonished to take a cake to their mothers or to a special service in church to honor their mothers. In Sweden, the cake was a waffle and in some parts of England a wafer, both cakes being baked on irons before the open fire. Then came the cakes in the form of a bun.

In England, the buns that were baked and eaten on Good Friday held a strange power. In some farm houses, a cake was hung with a string from the bacon rack over the fireplace. It remained for a whole year until it was replaced by a fresh one the next Good Friday. The bun was supposed to keep diseases away from the home. If an animal became sick,

Hot cross buns on Good Friday

a piece of the dry bun was powdered and put into warm mash and fed to the animal, who would be cured.

Christian missionaries tried to banish such superstitious ideas associated with the cakes by putting a cross of frosting upon them. This brought still another custom although not on the plane of the heathens. One custom was followed without fail, such as this: Two friends broke a bun in half in the cross, while standing within the doorway of the church on Good Friday morning before service. They said:

> Half for you and half for me,
> Between us two, Good-will shall be. Amen

As long as they kept the two halves, there never would be a quarrel.

The rule for buns of two generations ago reads: Rub four ounces of butter into two pounds of flour, four ounces of sugar, and a few caraway seeds if you like them. Put a spoonful of cream into a cup of yeast, and as much good milk as will make the above into a light paste; set it to rise and bake it on tins before a quick fire.

The bun has been the symbol for Good Friday since time immemorial. And the rhyme still lives on.

> Hot cross buns, hot cross buns,
> One a penny,
> Two a penny,
> Hot cross buns.

23

"THE WAY WE WASH OUR CLOTHES"

NOT TOO LONG AGO, YOUR GRANDMOTHER WAS STRUGGLING WITH A WASH
tub and a wooden scrubbing board. (There are many such in museums.)
Perhaps the tub was filled with water from the pump and heated on top
of the stove in a copper wash boiler. Perhaps it was filled with water toted
from the well and then heated. Quite often, it was water taken from the
rain barrel standing under the spout at the corner of the house—rain
water is a wonderful whitener. Home-made soap was soft soap, dipped
out of a barrel and of course made by the housewife herself, in the spring
of the year. The clothes were hung on a hemp line strung from post to post
out in the yard. Sometimes, the clothes were hung on the porch to avoid
any sudden shower. And sometimes the pieces were laid on the grass to
whiten.

Rinsing in fresh water was just as important as the first washing.
From the old country, the idea of leaching was carried out. After the
clothes had been washed they were put into a tub that had holes in the
bottom. Leaching water had been prepared ahead of the time for washing. A tub was filled with ashes from the fireplace and water was poured
over them. As it came through a hole in the tub, it contained akali.
Strained of all particles, it was poured over the clothes waiting in the tub.
The leaching water trickled out the holes of the tub, bleaching the clothes
as it rinsed them. Then the clothes were wrung out and hung to dry. It
was a long process, from the making of the bleaching water to the hanging of the clothes.

Clothes pins were hand-made from a stick of beech or maple wood
and they measured as much as eight inches long. Considering the weight
of the homespun sheets and blankets, clothes pins had to be long and
sturdy. Some pins were turned on the lathe and finished by hand with an
augur and jackknife. My collection of them counts up to about fifty, from
those over 150 years old to those nearly 100 years old.

The way we wash our clothes

Monday was wash-day and this was the nursery game, acted out by
us children:

> This is the way we wash our clothes,
>   wash our clothes, wash our clothes,
> This is the way we wash our clothes
>   on a Monday morning.

The clothes had to be sprinkled and rolled up the same afternoon. We
have an old tin sprinkler that must be 75 years old and antique shops
delight in showing you such an old tin can, with a handle and holes in the
cover.

Tuesday was ironing day!

> This is the way we iron our clothes,
>   iron our clothes, iron our clothes;
> This is the way we iron our clothes
>   on a Tuesday morning!

Then the heavy flatirons were brought down from the shelf, sad-irons,
weighing five, six, and seven pounds each. Four or sometimes only three
were set into an iron holder on top of the stove. A thick cloth holder lay
in waiting for the process of ironing, because the heat of the iron was
hot to the hands. A flatiron stand was brought out from a drawer to rest
the iron on between strokes. Those have become collectors' items.

The first irons were called box-irons. A box frame with a handle held an iron lug inside a trap door that lifted in grooves. The lug was heated in the fire on the hearth and then placed inside the box-iron, making the iron hot. Several lugs were heating to take the place of the cold one. Crimping irons came at the time of the open fire. These had two parts, a stationary bottom that was heated in the fire and a top that rocked or rolled in the corrugations of the base. These were used to crimp or plait the ruffles that were on the blouses worn by men.

A gauffering iron was another strange implement for pressing in the old days. It consisted of a long tube on a standard and a tool with an iron head on a handle with a wooden tip. The tool was heated in the fire and thrust into the tube. This made the tube hot. The little mob caps and bonnets were then pressed back and forth on the tube in the process of being ironed. Some gauffering irons had three tubes of different sizes.

A later iron for the stove top was one with a soapstone base, with an iron bottom. It had an iron handle fastened to the soapstone. Soapstone held the heat longer than iron.

Your grandmother's mother did not have even a wash tub. She had a barrel, filled with rain water and soft soap jelly. After the clothes had been put in, she used an implement called a pounder. It had a long handle and a heavy head. The head was filled with holes to make for suction as it was lifted up and down in the barrel. Every man made his own pounder and every one in my collection is different. The principle of it was to have a heavy head for weight when pounding. The housewife's strong arms wrung out the clothes and hung them on tow lines with long wooden clothes pins.

Young grandmother had a washing machine when such a thing appeared. They were either turned by a crank or rocked by a handle. Some had an arm that swung back and forth, moving a contraption with wooden teeth about in the clothes. Or the contraption was turned by two arms. A patent washer came out, looking like a wringer. A large corrugated roller in a frame was turned by a crank, moving against a set of small rollers. The clothes were mangled as the crank was turned back and forth, half motion, and after a proper length of time, the clothes were rolled through. A tub had to be purchased with the washer-mangler, the two parts screwed together.

Still another odd piece is in the collection. It is marked "patented" and is made of iron. It looks not unlike a long egg beater, with a handle on a long shank and a crank. A suction cup of tin is connected with the gears to the crank and that was pumped up and down, working in the clothes. The cup has wire bars across the bottom to prevent the clothes from being sucked in. At the top is a vent, a forerunner of the first principle of suction. A stick in a socket on the shank can be adjusted, dropped for a few clothes, or raised for many. Truly it seems one of a kind!

Great-grandmother's ironing was called smoothing or mangling. She had a long, narrow, and thin plank of wood, with corrugations on one side and a handle either on top or projecting at the end. With that was a wooden roller. Some rollers are tapered and others are the same in diameter, measuring about 24 inches in length. A sheet was folded four times and rolled over the stick. Then it was laid on the table and pushed back and forth with the smoothing board. This was done when the sheet was a bit damp, so the rolling both smoothed it and dried it. There is a short stick that evidently was made for pillow cases, which were folded only twice. The washing and ironing tools in a collection make a large group.

In the 20th century washing and ironing is another story. Machines have taken away the back-breaking procedure of wash-days and ironing days. If the various washing, drying, and mangling implements were listed here, it would sound like an advertisement sheet!

A window display of my washing and ironing implements in an electric appliance store attracted large crowds of both men and women. They gazed in wonder at the hand-made gadgets and visualized the labors involved. Many were the comments.

What a luxurious feeling you have when you drive into a "drive-in" laundry and leave a bag of soiled clothes! Then in three days, you drive back for the clean clothes. You may have a wet wash or have any and all parts starched and ironed or merely mangled. And laundry marts have sprung up in all sections. Here, you leave your bag of washing in the morning and call for it in the late afternoon, either wet or mangled. You can even do it yourself.

Such is the evolution of washing and ironing, from the days of the early Colonists to the present.

24

CANDLE MAKING IN THE OLD DAYS

WHEN THE COLONISTS BEGAN A NEW LIFE ON THESE SHORES, THE MEANS of a light after darkness was found in pine knots and pine splinters, and from the oil of the cod in the ocean. The knots and splinters were put into holders as they burned and gathering them in the fall of the year from dead trees became a necessity. Oil was burned in cup holders of various sorts. The history of burning fluids goes from the oil of cod to the oil of the sperm whale, to camphene to kerosene.

It was many years before candles were to be had, even though they had been used in the old country. In the 16th century, an English poet wrote in his book, *Directions to Housewives*:

> Wife, make thine own candle,
>   Spare penny to handle.
> Provide for thy tallow ere frost cometh in
> And make thine own candles ere Winter begins.

After Governor Winthrop arrived in Massachusetts, he wrote back to his wife in England to bring candles with her when she came over. And the Colonists sent for tallow and wicks so they could make candles.

There was no fat to be had for tallow in those first lean years because the few domestic animals were not slaughtered; rather were they needed to supply milk for butter and cheese. Deer suet, bear grease, and moose fat were often utilized in making those first candles. And farmers kept bees so as to have the wax for candles. When cattle increased and could be killed for eating, it was then that every bit of fat was saved and used for both candles and soap.

Wicks were made from the coarse part of flax, called tow, spun on the flax wheel. Even the silky milkweed could be spun into strands for wicks when there was no flax in the lean years.

Fat that had been saved during the winter months was clarified or "tried out" in a big kettle hanging on the crane. The tallow was skimmed off and put into another kettle where it was scalded again and skimmed a second time. The kettle was half filled with boiling water and the melted tallow.

Two slender rods, 25 or more inches long, were placed on the tops of two chair backs, turned back to back. Across those rods were placed six or eight shorter rods, candle rods or candle sticks. An old nursery rhyme has sprung from those sticks:

> Jack be nimble, Jack be quick,
> Jack jump over the candle stick.

The tow wicking had been wound into large balls ready to be used for the candle dipping. Some housewives took a nine-inch board and wound the tow on it, with as many loops as the board would hold. Then the loops were cut at the edge of the board, making lengths eighteen inches long. One of these was twisted double over a candle rod, making a wick nine inches long. A curious home invention is in my collection, coming from a home where several generations made candles for trade. It looks like a small bench, with a top board and two side boards. This rested over the knees. Fastened upright at one end is a razor blade. At the other end, nine inches away, is a long peg. The tow was wound around the razor blade and the peg, as much as could be held. Then, by sawing the strands against the razor, the tow was cut and the many strands of eighteen inches were ready to be twisted for a wick. For a long candle which was often made for the altar, the peg on the bench could be set farther away in another hole.

On each short candle rod, six or eight strands of tow were twisted. The strands were looped over the rod with the fingers first dipped in tallow, the better to hold them as they were twisted. This made a twisted strand of a little less than nine inches long, the length of the finished candle.

The kettle of tallow was swung out into the room or sometimes the tallow was poured into another kettle or tub and carried away from the heat of the fire. One rod of sticks was dipped into the kettle and replaced, a second was dipped and replaced, the process being continued until all the wicks had been dipped. By that time, the first set had hardened and the dipping continued until the candles were of the proper size. Each time more wax adhered to the candle. Within fifteen or twenty minutes, the candles were hard enough to slide off the rods. They were smoothed of any imperfections and hung up by their loops to finish drying. The candles were kept in the attic in a wooden box with sliding cover. A few

Candle-making in the old days

at a time were taken out, trimmed of the loops and put into the long, tin candle box that hung by the chimney. The various candle holders were filled every day from that box. Old diaries tell us that one candle burned about four hours.

The holders commonly used were of tin, some of them with a sliding floor that raised the candle as it burned down. Some holders were short and others were tall. Some had a base that curved upwards and some curved downwards. Those that curved downwards were said to have been used to scrape the hog of its bristles, for the edge was sharp and strong. Brass candle holders were brought from across the water; they were very beautiful and often made in pairs. Glass ones were made at the time of glass factories and they often had a glass circular ring from which hung glass prisms.

It has been aptly said that "necessity is the mother of invention." Two things that were made when candles came into use were the pickwick and the snuffer. The idea of the pickwick was to have a sharp point to pick up the wick when it drooped or sputtered. It was a small affair, having a steel pin in a handle, which set into a holder. When closed, it looks like a tiny standard, slender, two inches high. I have one of wood, which is rare, but they were made of copper, brass, and ivory. My adopted grandmother told of picking up wicks with a pin to make them burn brighter.

The snuffer was made to snuff out a candle, preventing it from smoking or spilling, as it might if blown out. The first snuffers were tin, conical in shape like a dunce's cap, about two inches high with a tiny loop handle. One in my collection is of wood. Other snuffers were made like pincers or scissors to snuff out the flame, generally made of steel. Some were of silver and one I have is of tin. These always rested on a tin tray, the length of the snuffer.

When tin came into use for domestic articles, tin candle molds were made, and candles were no longer dipped. The common molds were nine inches long, tapering, with a support at the bottom. At one side is a long handle by which it was held when the tallow was poured in. Molds were also put into a wooden frame, standing on bracket legs. These molds were of pewter, tin, or Bennington pottery, often as many as three or four dozen in a frame.

Altar candles were taller and larger in size. The molds were generally made single, but occasionally double. A recent find was a wooden mold inside a tin altar mold, the same shape, including the point. This leads me to believe that all tin candle molds were made and soldered on a wooden mold. How else could they be so perfect in shape, the seam soldered, the tip added, without having a mold to shape it on?

There is an art in stringing the molds with wicking. A tin mold was strung by running the wick down and tying it at the bottom, or running it back and forth through all the molds. At the top, a wooden or metal skewer held each loop. One came to me all strung.

After the tallow was poured, the candles were allowed to harden. Then the mold was quickly dipped into hot water, the knots were cut and the skewers lifted, bringing up the candles. The large wooden holder had a long skewer across the length of the top, each row having a skewer. When hardened, the candles could be lifted and hung to dry. There were many contraptions that were used in drying, one looking like the ribs of an umbrella inverted, on which each candle had a separate rib. This was nothing but a limb shaped with projections.

The candles were smoothed of any imperfection and then laid away in a large wooden box. The typical candle box has a sliding cover and holds many dozen candles. The tin candle box with a hasp in its cover hung near to the fireplace, holding the few that would be used from day to day. The loops were snipped off before the candle was set into its holder.

For pouring tallow, often there was a tin scoop, with three, four, or five spouts. The spouts were placed the same distance apart as the distance of the molds in the frame. Holding a quart or more of tallow, many molds could be filled at one time. Without the scoop, the tallow was poured with a small tin cup.

Many times the job of making candles was given to an itinerant candle-maker in those early days. He went from house to house, carrying his own molds. In return for his work, the candle-maker was given his lodging and meals, or, as they said, his "board and keep." He was given fat or suet or even tallow to take away with him, which he made into candles to barter for commodities for himself.

On the coast, a shrub was found that was called a bayberry bush. In Sweden, it was called the tallow shrub and in England the candleberry bush. Each berry was coated with a grey wax that had a fragrant odor, like incense. The berries were gathered in the autumn. Boiling them brought the wax to the surface and this was skimmed off and put into another kettle with water, to be used for dipping. One bushel of berries made four pounds of wax. The candles gave out a fragrance and burned slower and brighter than the common tallow. Bayberries were used before tallow from animal fat had become plentiful. For one candle, it took a bushel of berries.

So important were the berries, a law was passed in 1687 at Long Island, stating that berries could not be picked until September 15, under the penalty of a fine.

Bayberry candles are still made from the bayberry bush that continues to grow in profusion. It is a popular custom to burn such a candle on New Year's Eve.

Burn a candle to the socket,
You will have health, wealth and money in your pocket.

25

GONE IS THE OLD APPLE BARREL

A REPORT CAME DOWN FROM NOVA SCOTIA ABOUT THE PLIGHT OF THE barrel makers. The barrel appears to be doomed, going along with the Country Store and the General Post Office, the Country Doctor, the horse and buggy, and the old phonograph and stereoscope. Yes, call it Progress. Something else takes its place and other methods and ways step up as the years go by. We have to go along, too, or be left behind.

Another thing of the past is the wagon that carried new barrels, from the coopers' shops to the local hardware stores. Some cooper shops that make buckets, tubs, and bowls still flourish in New England—but no barrels! The barrel wagon had side posts and end posts, each holding an inverted barrel. Inside the row of posts, more barrels were stacked, making a load that looked big, although, it was light. One horse drew such a wagon as it came to town to sell the load. There was an old saying, "See a load of barrels, sign of rain."

A barrel of sugar and a barrel of flour were common in homes up to 1900. Places to keep the barrels were built in the old pantries, with a lid that lifted up; when closed the lid was part of the pantry shelf. Some pantries had a round platform that held the barrel and it could be revolved to bring it out into the pantry when needed. Buying half a pound of sugar a week during the World Wars brought to mind the days of my childhood when the family had a barrel of sugar and a barrel of flour and barrels of apples.

When Father and Mother set up housekeeping in our big house, they bought four barrels of apples that first winter. They both liked apples! No fancy apples but the various winter apples to be made into pies, dumplings, apple sauce, and apple butter—as well as the kinds to eat. Mother recalls that she was picking over apples most of the winter, even though the barrels were kept in our cold storeroom!

Then Father planted our big yard with fruit trees, grape vines, black-

Gone is the old apple barrel

berries, and strawberries. Cherries, plums, quinces, pears, and apples were
soon plentiful and the summer and fall seasons saw much canning going
on in the big kitchen. The apples were Greenings, Gravensteins, and Red
Astrachans. The Greenings could be stored but the others were eaten
during the season, as well as put up in canning jars. A lot of care but such
wealth!

I well remember the apple dumplings with sauce poured over them.
And a great favorite with us children was the pie that had no bottom
crust, and was turned over when served with rich, heavy cream. It is
called a deep-dish apple pie today. And I remember the cherry pie that
was made with strips for the top crust, lattice work. Yes, we had rhubarb,
too, and that went into pies. We had a small cherry tree and that bore
heavily; tart red cherries. We had a lot of fun picking them and eating
them, but when it came to canning time, Mother often had to hire a
neighbor boy to do the picking!

The old cellars always had a cold storeroom. There were shelves and
a rack for the vinegar keg and space for apples and this and that. I have
heard Mother tell about the time our maid poured the vinegar into a tub
and washed the inside of the barrel, because "it had some awful thick stuff
in it!" That was the mother that had collected and which was quite necessary to make good vinegar. Our storeroom today is still a part of our

cellar, but there is no vinegar keg and no barrel of apples, but plenty of this and that.

The modern homes do not plan for storage any more. It is not a cellar any more; it is a basement or a playroom. The families cannot store any more except perhaps in a garage which is not always cold. So the only recourse is to buy apples in small quantities, even at six cents apiece. Today's apples are highly cultivated, there are many new ones that have been developed by means of much scientific research. A friend told me that her husband had taken twenty years to develop a special kind. Apples are large, juicy, and tempting. Many orchards have storage plants, so we can buy the year around.

Little wonder then that the barrels of apples are gone and even the barrels themselves.

26

FALL TIME IS APPLE TIME

AS CHILDREN, WE COULD NEVER WAIT UNTIL APPLES RIPENED. WE WOULD take a green apple and not give a thought to the consequences. I remember up country there was a russet apple tree. Our vacation ended before the apples were ripe and ready to pick, every year we would taste a green one—out behind the barn—and every year we would go home without knowing how a russet tasted when ripe.

What a variety of apples we have today! Orchards are scientifically cultivated and the fruit has been crossed and perfected. A story came to me of a young man who had graduated from a State College and gone back to his father's farm. He asked his father if he might work on the apple orchard and bring it up to a perfection it had never known. The father would not give his consent as he did not believe in any new ideas. But when the son asked for a part of the orchard to experiment with, the father gave him a corner. When fall came and the apples on the trees in the son's part were perfect and large, the father had to acknowledge that there must be something worthwhile in the new ways.

Apple time is cider time. In the early days, the common drink in the morning, at noon, and at night was cider, even for the children. After apple trees had been brought to the new country and had begun to bear well, cider was made from them. Cider was so important it was put into wills. If a man did not have six or eight barrels to bequeath to his widow, he was not considered much of a success. One man who died in 1761 provided in his will that his widow should be supplied with five barrels of cider annually.

With no means of keeping apples through the winter, various ways of using them were followed. Nearly every family dried their apples. This was done by paring and coring them and cutting them into slices. These were dried on racks in the sunshine or over heat from the fireplace or stove. Those hooks we find in the ceiling over the hearth were put there to hold the racks for drying sliced apples. The apples could also be quartered after they were pared and then threaded on a stout thread. These strings were dried over racks similar to clothes racks. Dried apples were kept in boxes until they were to be used for pies or puddings.

Making applesauce was another way of using apples. It was called boiled applesauce and the rule reads thus: "Ten gallons of cider, three pecks of apples, cored and quartered, ten pounds of sugar and five ounces of cinnamon." Both sweet and sour apples were used in the kettle. Sometimes, molasses was added, the maple molasses that came from the drippings of maple sugar. The fire under the kettle was very hot and we read that a layer of straw was put on the bottom of the kettle to keep the sauce from burning. When done, it was a thick, syrupy paste. It was stored in barrels for the winter.

Fall time is apple time

Apple butter was still another way of using the apples. Out in Pennsylvania, they have a festival at the time of making apple butter. It is called a "lettwarrik party." It is a community affair with the neighbor women paring the apples. It takes bushels and bushels of apples. Paring is done by hand, but apple parers of wood and iron vouch for the fact that much hand labor could be saved by using mechanical devices. The rule for apple butter calls for five gallons of cider to one bushel of peeled and quartered apples, and five pounds of sugar. Some families out there in Pennsylvania add spice, enough to suit the taste. The cider is put into huge kettles over a hot fire. It has to be a copper kettle, for iron turns the apples black. When the cider begins to boil, a white froth appears on the top. This is skimmed off and the apples dropped in. After the apples begin to darken, the sugar is added. The mixture must be stirred constantly to prevent it from burning. And if it comes to the point of boiling over, a piece of butter is added to quiet it.

The fires are so hot the workers cannot stand near the kettle. In Pennsylvania, they have a long-handled stirrer with a paddle head at right angles. In the head are holes through which the mixture flows as the stirrer is moved back and forth. The worker stands outside the house and reaches with the stirrer through a window. One such stirrer is in my collection. It measures nine feet long, with a head of 30 inches. When I bought this from a dealer out on the Berkshire Trail, I was told that a stirrer 12 feet long had just been sold. The stirrer rests on the edge of the kettle, taking the weight off the worker. My stirrer has worn grooves about two feet back from the head, showing where it dragged back and forth on the edge of the kettle. That would make the kettle approximately three feet in diameter. Apple butter can be cooked slowly all day, or rapidly in four hours.

Some kettles were built in a brick enclosure, with place for a fire underneath. The same kettle was used for mash and for clothes on wash day, as well as for making apple butter or apple sauce. In some museums, one finds an apparatus of wood that fitted into a large kettle and which was used when making apple butter, a frame that has paddles that are turned by a crank.

The Shakers made both applesauce and apple butter and sold them commercially. Inventories show that this occupation was carried on into the 19th century. The price for a barrel of applesauce ranged around $12 in 1846. The Shakers had an apple-drying house, a kiln, where they dried their apples. The heating apparatus was on the ground floor and places for racks were on the second floor.

We hear very little today about making applesauce and apple butter. Every housewife makes a lot of apple sauce but we never have to freeze it and pack it away in barrels. We can always buy applesauce in cans, and apple butter can be had in jars. Years ago, an apple orchard was a valuable contribution to good living, and it still is today.

27

THE SATURDAY NIGHT BATH

HOW FEW THERE ARE WHO REMEMBER THE BIG WOODEN TUB THAT WAS dragged from the woodshed and set in front of the kitchen range, filled with hot water from the teakettle and used for the weekly bath! It was probable that a wooden tub was used even before the days of stoves, coming into existence at the time of the huge fireplaces and filled with water from the iron teakettle that hung on the crane.

The Saturday night bath was a weekly occasion. There was not much fun in it, if we go by reports. Imagine a not-too-warm kitchen, the tub partly filled with not-too-hot water, and a cake of homemade soap that sank to the bottom of the tub. Mother helped all of the children and saw

Saturday night bath

109

to it that a thorough job was done. It is easy to think that more than one child stood in the tub at the same time.

I have a tub like those used for the Saturday night bath. It stands thirty inches high and has a diameter of a little less than three feet. In comparison to the ordinary tub, the size is large. I bought it at an auction up country, and a friend took it home in his beach wagon. At a much later time, it was borrowed by a group of stock players for their performance of *The Cotter's Saturday Night*. The leading man was amazed at finding such a tub, the largest one he had ever seen.

Real bathtubs put in their appearance by the beginning of the nineteenth century. But they were far from the style of a bathtub of the twentieth century. Those first tubs were made of wood and lined with tin. They stood on casters so they could be wheeled about and there was a cock for letting out the water. One such tub once stood in a small room in Gore Hall in Waltham, the brick mansion of Governor Gore of Massachusetts. Overhead was a hole in the floor with an extending tube. As the master sat in the tub, a servant overhead poured down warm water upon him. Such a performance was probably not indulged in often.

Among my papers is a clipping quoting Dr. Cecil Drinker, former dean of the Harvard School of Public Health. Dr. Drinker said that according to the diary of his great grandmother's, a bathtub appeared in Philadelphia in 1803. The diary read:

"My husband went into ye tepid bath before dinner. He hansel'd [an old word meaning 'to use for the first time' as found in the dictionary] a new bathing tub bought yesterday for $17, made of wood, lined with tin and painted, with casters under ye bottom and a brass cock to let out the water." A friend tells me that her great grandmother had such a tub in Philadelphia and the neighbors all came in to see it.

Another type of bathtub was a folding one. It stood in a high cabinet and when it was to be used, it was let down onto the floor. Two short legs dropped into place in the front end. How the water was put in and how it was let out is a matter of conjecture. Still another seems to be part of a sofa. The bottom part of the frame pulled out and in that was a tin bathtub. Again, water had to be carried in and taken out. Both of these tubs were lined with tin.

Coming to the time of sitz tubs and sitz baths, the market had a variety to offer. One in my family was like a big deep armchair, resting on the floor. It was painted green on the outside and a cream color on the inside. The patient sat in this, his feet extending onto the floor and covered with a blanket. Our tub was given to the drive for metals during World War I.

Another type of sitz tub was quite common 75 and more years ago.

It was a large inverted hat, four feet across. The user sat on a built-up seat on the rim. There was a small space for the soap and a hole out of which the water was poured. Such a tub was used for colds, fevers and any and all minor sicknesses, besides being brought out for the Saturday night bath.

A type of smaller proportions was a foot tub. The patient sat in a chair with his feet in the tub, covered with a warm blanket. These were found in porcelain as well as in tin.

When I began collecting woodenware, I had an elderly friend who told me many a story of the old days. She said her father used to have headaches. The family saw an advertisement in a Boston paper that told of a shower bath that would help cure headaches and many other ills. They sent for it and rigged it up in the attic. It consisted of a frame covered with a curtain, and across the top were cross pieces of iron. The patient was supposed to stand in the tub. A can of water with an opening that was controlled by a cord was placed on the top cross piece. When the patient pulled the cord, the water would pour down upon his head, as he stood in the tub. All went well until the cold water struck the father's head. With one whoop, he dashed out from the curtain, down the attic stairs and into his bedroom, all the while uttering curses. Mother and daughter stood by convulsed with laughter; they felt a bit chagrined, too. No mention was ever made of that patent shower again.

While doing research work on tin, I chanced on the story of a patent shower, a tin can with holes in the bottom and a handle that released the water. Soon after finding the story and picture, I visited an antique shop owned by a friend. Before I had reached the doorstep, she came to the door exclaiming over her latest find. I went into the house and there before my eyes was the shower bath can like the one I had seen pictured. With an exclamation of delight, I took it out of her hands and explained to her what it was. We went to her sink, experimented with the intake of the water and the release, and found how it worked. It had a patent on it of August 1, 1869. The patient was supposed to press a lever that released the water as he held the can over his head. It appeared to be the same patented shower can that was tried out up in the attic those many years ago.

When plumbing came into the home, a tin bathtub was installed in the bathroom. Long, narrow, and deep, it was set in sheathing that matched that of the room, with its boxed-in wash bowl and boxed-in toilet. It is a safe conjecture that not a few homes still have such an arrangement.

It is a far cry from that first huge wooden tub that was dragged in from the woodshed to the beautiful modern bathtubs and shower baths of this mid-twentieth century. And in the transition, the ritual of the Saturday night tub has passed.

28

THE FAMILY DININGROOM COMES BACK

"MY DAUGHTER IS HAVING A DINING ROOM IN HER NEW HOUSE." SO SAID a friend of mine. "She wouldn't be happy in a house without a dining room because she has always had one."

A short time previous to that remark, I saw an account in the paper from the Associated Press telling of the comeback of the dining room. Stores are promising a return of the importance of buying furniture, linens, silverware, and glassware. The tide always seems to turn if we wait long enough.

Back in the time when the settlers hewed their own timber and made their own homes and furnishings, the table on which the family ate was a thick wide board plank, resting on trestles. Lack of space in the one room which served all purposes brought about the need of setting away the table after each meal—taking the board off the trestle and standing it against the wall.

Long years afterward when there were many rooms in a house and the dining room was an important room, the expressions "table board" and "board and room" were often heard. These sprung up from the time when the plank board was used as a table. "Table board" came to mean the meals served on the table and "board and room" meant meals and room. And "boarders" were people who ate, literally, from the boards. These words still remain in common usage.

For convenience, the table developed so that it could be changed in size. First came the gate-legged table of many legs put together in sections as a gate. This could be closed by swinging the legs back and dropping the leaves. Tables came with extension leaves, to accommodate a small family or a large family. These were at first mahogany, then there was a period of black walnut, followed by the coming to popularity of oak.

Each period saw a change in the contents of the dining room. The mahogany era had a beautiful table, long, low sideboards, side tables, and chairs made by master craftsmen. Crystal chandeliers hung from the ceiling and soft candlelight from silver candelabras shone on beautiful china, glass, and silver, priceless possessions of well-to-do families. This room saw much formal entertaining.

The family dining room

The Gay Nineties brought an era of black walnut; extension tables, marble top tables and cane seated chairs, with a marble top sideboard that had a large mirror and side shelves on the upper part. It was then that hanging lamps with colored shades were in vogue, raised and lowered as needed. It was then that the family used the dining room as a room in which to gather at any time of the day or evening. Comfortable chairs, often a sofa, and a combination bookcase and desk were used for ornamental dishes and knickknacks, while the desk was a place for the family to write, catch up on accounts or do "home-work." And tall cabinets with curved glass doors for dishes were in evidence. A blackboard for the children hung on the wall or stood on an easel, a canary bird was in a cage at the window, and quite often there was a basket for the new-born kittens. All of this gave an air of folksiness, a home. That was emphasized by a cross-stitch motto over the door, GOD BLESS OUR HOME.

Another generation gave way to the mandates of architects in building a house with an alcove for a dining room or merely setting off one end of a long sitting room for tables, chairs, and a small dresser. Built-in settles were placed in the kitchen, or else a snack bar sufficed. This was for the convenience of the busy family who seemed to flourish under the tension and haste, each unto his own business. Gone was the family life and gone was the dining room with its table covered with snowy white linen and sparkling glassware and silverware.

So we rejoice at the comeback of the old-fashioned dining room. We oldsters like to think how we gathered in that central room of the house, sitting around a well-filled table, entertaining friends in a leisurely way or playing games on the cleared table after the evening meal. We have memories that can never be taken away from us. Let's hope the architects and the merchants will bring back the dining room, the gathering place of the family.

29

WHEN TIME WAS FIGURED BY THE SUN:
PEG CALENDARS AND NOONMARKS

RESPONDING TO THE DOOR BELL ONE EVENING, I FOUND A COLLECTOR-
friend standing there, eager to show me something. "Here is an old peg
calendar and if you don't want it, our friend will. He has a small one."

Every collector knows there is always something he has never seen
and which he sooner or later becomes interested in. I listened attentively
while my collector-friend explained that there were 31 holes in the thin
strip of wood and each hole represented a day of the month. A wooden
peg like that of the shoe cobbler was used to move along from day to day.

Of course I bought it and after he had gone, I examined my new
acquisition carefully. About nine inches long, two inches wide, tapering
to the top, it had hung by a leather strap. At that end, there was a label
written in ink, now faded.

On the back of the calendar, an inscription was written in pencil, which
is hard to decipher. "John Dagi's Almanack A Fernandos Florida Days
of the month." On the front, the label reads—

"Given by Abbie Johnson Whiting who received it from an old slave
while she was at work for the freedom. A. C. Stoddard, 1875."

The calendar lay with my collection and at times was admired and
explained. One day, a letter came from someone interested in early history

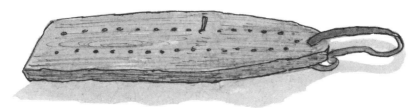

Time by the peg calendar

and she told me of reading in a book about how time was told by the sun, mentioning "noonmarks." That was a new word to me.

Talking with a rare friend who has stores of information, I mentioned noonmarks and my peg calendar. She had lived at one time in Mississippi and had come in contact with life of the plantation owners. She told of the slaves who owned peg calendars; they all seemed to have them. Her recollection was of the peculiar need they filled. When a baby was expected, the mother began to use the calendar—one month along, two months along, and on to the ninth month.

Besides the small board for the days of the month, there was one for the days of the week. It was an ingenious way to use a piece of wood, and a peg, but it would be a bit difficult to keep track of the direction the peg should be moved!

That word noonmark was quoted from the furniture book of N. Hudson Moore; "the noonmark on the window ledge which may be seen today on some of the old houses still standing." Writing to the Wayside Inn, she learned that no window ledge showed any mark. It was my conclusion immediately that it would be a farm house where such a mark was found for they had no time piece in those early days. It would be marked on a sunny window sill in the South side of the house. Even at that, noontime would be variable!

I recalled the Rollo books of my youth. We had the Rollo books, the Jonas Books, and the Prudy books; and they now repose in the library in Oakham, Massachusetts. Rollo discovered the movement of the sun and made a mark on the floor by the big barn door.

From such primitive ways of marking the movement of the sun came the sun dial. Recorded in *The Century Book of Facts*: "Sun dials were invented 558 B.C. The first in Rome 308 B.C. was that erected by Papirius Cursor, when time was divided into hours."

Anyone could go far in studying time and the many creations that followed. There is always somebody interested in some part of early living—even to a rat trap, which was mentioned in one of my letters!

PART II
IN THE PARLOR

30

HAIR-CLOTH SOFAS WERE ONCE POPULAR

CHILDHOOD MEMORIES ARE OFTEN STRANGE AND UNACCOUNTABLE! YET they are real, and as we grow older they color our lives.

Down toward Lincoln Square on Main Street in my native town, our family physician had an office. The double door of two panels with etched ground glass was directly on the level of the sidewalk. This led into the waiting room.

Shall I ever forget the first day I was taken as a child to see the kindly doctor! The room was furnished attractively with pictures on the walls and magazines on the table. But nothing stands out in my mind more than the haircloth sofa.

In those days of the Gay Nineties, sofas and chairs of black walnut with horsehair seats were very common. They came in sets; sofa, two side chairs, a father chair, and a mother chair. The carving was of three types; roses, grapes, and lines called "fingers," some very elaborate with much carving and others more plain. Today, they are much sought after and they bring high prices.

In the doctor's office, the sofa with the haircloth had a high and rounded seat. Mother lifted me up onto it and I promptly slid off. That began the fun! I climbed up again and slid off, up and down. I forgot all about the long wait while busying myself with sliding.

Today, a grown woman, my mind turns to the haircloth on that sofa. Because I have haircloth sieves in my collection, I became interested in the process of using animal hair.

Horsehair was taken from the tail and the mane of the horse. Thus there were shades of brown, black, and gray. That of the tail was the most valuable, described as hard, while that of the mane was inferior and called soft. Further than that, "live" hair taken from a live animal commanded the highest price as against "dead" hair from a dead animal.

There were three sortings of the hair, length, color, and quality. The hair was washed in a warm soap bath to which lime or potash had been added. Then the hair went through a bleaching process by means of the juice of logwood. Lastly, it was dyed.

Long hair was combed on steel combs, separated into different lengths and thicknesses, three feet being the longest. In my collection is what had been named incorrectly as a hetchel, for combing flax. It is a narrow board plank into which were driven steel nails, standing about five inches high. The nails form a square of about six inches. Unlike the hetchel for use in flax, this one has a second plank, the size of the bottom one, which screws with heavy wooden screws down onto the nails. Research work brought about the fact that this type was used when sorting and straightening hair, the board clamped hard onto the points of the nails, holding the hair from slipping out.

Hair-cloth sofas were once popular

From the long horsehair, cloth was woven, the width of the cloth being determined by the length of the hair. Strong linen or cotton twist formed the warp, the length of the cloth to be woven. Short horsehair was and is used for stuffing for seats of sofas and chairs and saddles. It was not always pure, but mixed with cowhair and pighair. Today a manufacturer states that it is 20 per cent horsehair—or cowhair—and 80 per cent hog hair. The strands were made curly by a process of twisting, then soaked several hours in cold water and baked in an oven. Open any chair stuffing and see how stiff and curly the hair is. Pillows and mattresses should have pure animal hair.

Up in the Farmer's Museum in Old Hadley, Massachusetts, I found a loom for making mats for horsehair sieves. The loom stands five feet high and on it can be woven a mat about 14 or 15 inches square. One such mat lay beside the loom and with it several bunches of horsehair. The strands were about 15 inches long, the bundle being two inches in diameter, tied with coarse tow or cord. When making a sieve, the worker had a stool with a top the size of that of the finished sieve. With the stool was a metal cover with a handle. The finished mat was placed on the stool, the cover pressed down onto it and the edges were bound around with a coarse thread. Two hoops had been made for each sieve, one a bit smaller than the other. They were the exact size of the top of the stool and the mat. The finished mat was clamped between the two hoops, fitting together very tight.

The Shakers made sieves extensively, and in any Shaker Museum there are working parts for making them.

In Old Hadley, there were two sisters who made sieves to sell, using that loom in the Museum. They were the Marsh sisters and they lived several generations ago. A brother lived with them. They must have been very eccentric for they kept their shades drawn and never left the house. The brother sold the sieves to neighboring towns so that the family might have money to buy provisions.

In my collection are several horsehair sieves, varying in size from two to 15 inches in diameter. The small ones were used to sift powdered herbs for medicines or for spices, first crushed in a mortar with a pestle. I have a nest that came from a doctor's office, some of horsehair and some of finely woven silk. Another material that was woven into mats for sieves was the cockle, a weed that grows among grain. This is coarse and light in color. An unusual sieve came into my possession and upon analysis, I found it had a mat of cockle weed. Then I learned that the Shakers often used that for their sieves, which convinced me that I had a Shaker sieve.

The large sieves were used in the kitchen to sift flour and meals. Two of my sieves have a plaid weave in the mat, a mixture of two colors of hair. It could have been from horses' tails or from the tails of a horse and a cow. Hair sieves were used many years before pierced tin could be had; later, wire sieves were used. One other type of sieve was made from a piece of calf skin, pierced with holes.

Cow hair went into plaster, mixed with crushed seashells and clay. This was in the days before lime was discovered in the soil. The first use of plaster was just before the end of the 17th century, but then only a few families plastered a room or two to help keep out the cold. By another half century, plaster was commonly used.

Cow hair was mixed with other hair for stuffing and when bleached and dyed it went with wool for making blankets and felt for hats.

Camel hair and goat hair is used in making cloth and other textiles. In the camel, the hair was taken from the humps, the neck, and the legs.

Young animals have the finest. In the Bible we are told that coats were made of camel hair. Today, a camel's hair coat is of high value. Contrary to belief, the soft camel's hair brushes were never made from the hair of a camel, but rather from the tail of a sable or squirrel.

It is the angora or mohair goat that gives the best hair for textiles. There is a cashmere goat, too, whose hair is used in making fine shawls. The coarser hair of the camel and the goat is made into carpets, tent coverings, and other articles.

Pig hair is often mixed with hair for stuffing, but we think of brushes when we mention pig's bristles. It has been said that every part of the pig can be used but the squeal.

It is a long way back to the haircloth sofa and the horsehair sieves but we know that horsehair is still used in mattresses. And we enjoy our camel's hair coats and blankets and our dresses made from goat's hair.

31

WALL TO WALL CARPETS

ON THE TURNPIKE FROM WORCESTER TO BOSTON IS A HIGH SIGN READING, WALL TO WALL CARPETS. It is not surprising to see such a sign, for as sure as the sun rises and sets, so history repeats and fashions revert.

It does not seem long ago that carpets covered the floor; and in fact, many old homes have left them on, all these changing years. The patterns were large and gay, the larger and gayer the better. They corresponded to the furnishings of the room; ruffled sofa pillows, fancy over-stuffed chairs with gay coverings, a whatnot in one corner filled with ornaments and knickknacks, a small table in another corner with a red frilly worsted mat on which was a gilt box-frame holding a hair wreath, oil paintings on the wall, and heavy portierres at the doors. Such a room needed a gay carpet to complete the picture of color and gaiety.

It was about 1827 that floor coverings appeared. The names of the fine carpets were the same names as the places from which the carpets came; Saxony of England, Tournal of Belgium, and Brussels of Germany were the finest. Others were the Imperial, Wilton, Kidderminster of England, and those of Venetian and Scotch varieties. Oriental rugs were called Turkey Carpets. All these carpets came into vogue in 1840. Previous to that time, ingrain carpeting was used extensively—a soft, woven carpeting, the wool being dyed before it was woven. Women wove their own carpeting, too, from woolen rags.

Often at auctions, a tool comes up that seems to be a mystery to the average person. It is a carpet layer. It has two arms about 25 inches long, worked on a hinge. At the end of one arm is a set of metal teeth. When laying the carpet, the teeth caught into the edge of the carpet, which was then stretched out to the baseboard. This made the carpet tight and it was nailed to the floor. But before this could be done, rolls of paper wadding were put over the entire floor, as a padding.

A floor covering of different material came from China, known as

123

China matting or straw matting. This was used on floors before woolen carpeting appeared. And even when fine carpeting could be bought, straw matting continued to be used in bedrooms, hallways, and the maid's rooms. A padding with a thin layer of wool was always put under the matting. Straw matting was the bane of housekeepers! It could never be kept clean, for dirt sifted through the weaving and when such a matting was taken up, disgrace seemed to fall upon the housekeeper who saw the accumulated dirt.

Wall to wall carpets

To clean a carpeted room, there was no way but to sweep it. Inventions for cleaning had not appeared, the carpet sweeper coming some years later. The housewife tore up bits of soaked newspapers and scattered them over the entire room and then swept them up along with sweeping the carpet. The wet paper was supposed to absorb the dust to a certain degree. Even on a straw matting, such a performance was the only way to obtain necessary cleanliness. Remember how the housewife tied up her head with a cloth, wore a long apron with a ruffle at the bottom—a dust catcher— and long cuffs over her sleeves!

The word "drugget" appears in early history and I turned to my mother for information. In the dining room, under the table and chairs, a small rug of wool or linen was placed. This was to protect the rug and was also called a "crumb catcher." Another burden placed upon the housewife, to keep that small rug clean after each meal. Housewives and their maids seemed to expect to work from morn till night, because in the Victorian era, everything was cluttered, fussy and filly, forever needing care.

Perhaps carpets will be back again, laid from wall to wall. But with the modern cleaning devices, the burden of cleaning days will not be too severe. There is something about carpets in a room that promotes a homey look, something that hardwood floors cannot produce.

32

FROM THE QUILL TO THE BALL POINT PEN

THERE'S BEEN SUCH A RADICAL CHANGE IN WRITING EQUIPMENT, IT IS hard to believe the story of the evolution of writing.

Back in the prehistoric era, man's desire to write gave him the incentive to find a tool. He turned to the reed and he found he could inscribe his messages with various juices. Quills from wild birds were also adapted to the same use. A quill has a thin membrane of skin in which it is encased in the body of the bird. This was removed and the tip sharpened to make a point for the purpose of writing.

Civilized man used the same source for his writing, taking quills from wild turkeys and later from the domesticated goose. A goose could be plucked of its quills but once a year; doing so more often than that killed the bird.

The quill was whittled to a point, which was split to make it flexible. Some of the feathers were left on at the end for a handle. As the point dulled, it could be sharpened again. Age does not seem to cause the pen to deteriorate; I have one in my collection, along with the first holder for both pen and ink.

The holder is a round block of wood, stained, 4 inches in diameter and 1½ inches high. Three holes were cut near the edge to hold the pens and in the center is a small well for ink. Ink was made from nutgalls and sulphate or salt of iron. A nutgall is an excrescence on oak trees or leaves, and when it is crushed a dark liquid comes from it. Logwood, a tree from the West Indies, and the indigo plant were used for juices.

To dry the ink after writing on paper, sand was used as a blotter. Fine cut steel was also used. Wooden holders for sand or steel were manufactured and called sanders or sand shakers. The earliest ones were made of tin, then came those of wood, either maple or lignum vitae. They were shaped like an urn, flaring at the top and bottom. From tiny holes in the

An old-fashioned quill pen

top, the sand was scattered onto the writing and moved about, drying the ink. It was poured back into the sander for other writing.

China, glass, tin, wood, mother-of-pearl, and brass were used in making inkwells. Some were intended for traveling on board ships while others were decorative ornaments for a desk at home. One of tin, shaped as a cylinder, held a manuscript in one part and an inkwell at the other end. Another one, of tin, was a small trunk-like box, locked with a tiny key. The upper part held two bottles of ink. Sliding out the lower section, the end of which was the side of the trunk, revealed a small pen and sticks of sealing wax. A tiny holder for a tiny candle was at one end, for melting the wax. This complete outfit is said to have been used on board ship.

Another writing accessory was the stamper. These were made of ivory or brass, with a short handle, at the end of which was a seal or initials. After the wax was heated over a candle and allowed to drip onto the flap of the envelope, the stamper made the imprint and sealed the letter. The earliest letters had no envelopes but were folded and sealed with wax and a stamper.

An ivory piece in my collection, ten inches long and elaborately carved, is a combination of paper cutter and pen. Unscrewing one end produces a pen, with the cutter as a handle. A stamper is on the end opposite the cutter, the part that unscrews. In an opening below the stamper was once a miniature picture, viewed like transparent pictures of those early days.

Today, we have a ball point pen. Always ready and conveniently carried about, it does away with much fuss and trouble. Our names are on stickers and letter heads.

But colored sealing wax did add a bit of romance!

33

SHADOW BOXES AND GLASS DOMES

ONE OF THE MANY BEAUTIFUL PIECES OF HANDWORK CREATED A CENtury ago is the hair wreath that was put into a frame and hung on the parlor wall. To us of today, it is not a cheerful ornament to have on view. But if we look at it from the point of view of art, we find it a thing of beauty.

The various shades of hair were used, taken from the living as well as from the deceased. The hair was first washed and sorted. A wire foundation was made, not quite full circle, on which the flowers and leaves were fastened. Wire supported the hair flowers as well as the stems, petals, leaves, tendrils, and rosettes. Tiny colored beads were often put into the center of the flowers. These were grouped solidly around the wire foundation. According to the skill of the creator, so was the artistry of the work. The wreaths were both round and oval in shape, elaborately or simply made, of black hair, brown hair, gold, and gray.

The frames that held the wreath were walnut or rosewood, although many were of pine, gilded, which made a frame of light weight. They had a deep side wall, three or four inches wide, and painted white. Cardboard or heavy paper was put on as a back to which the wreath was attached. They were called recessed frames or box frames, and in recent years the name of shadow frames has been attached to them.

Hair work was exceedingly popular for a number of years, from the time following the Civil War until the so-called Gay Nineties. Much jewelry was made from hair. A book titled *The Art of Hair Work* was published in 1867, written by Mark Campbell.

Besides the wreaths of hair that were put into frames, there were those of wax, cloth, cotton, and feathers. The feathers were taken from various birds, dyed, and cut into shapes that made flowers and leaves. Cotton was colored and made to represent flowers and leaves, and cloth was done in a like manner. Each flower was fastened to the foundation with a wire.

On the wall of the dining room of a friend is a box frame that has half an openwork pottery dish fastened to the back, filled with wax fruit. It has a gold frame. Apples, pears, peaches, strawberries, blackberries, plums, apricots, tomatoes, cucumbers, peppers are all in natural color. The story of wax fruit is most interesting. This was another accomplishment of the Gay Nineties. In my collection are ten Plaster of Paris molds in which wax fruit was made. An ear of corn, a cucumber, walnuts, an apple, an orange, a plum, half a peach, a grape or cherry, a crabapple and an apricot; all were made in two parts.

The process of making the fruit or vegetable was to pour the liquid wax into half the mold, press the mold together, and shake it vigorously. This spread the wax into the entire mold. After a short time, the wax hardened, the mold was opened, and the fruit removed. Since the mold was made from the real fruit or vegetable itself, the wax was an exact duplicate. If the wax was mutton tallow, like that used in candle molds, the object would come easily out of the mold. Perhaps wax from bees or spermeceti might have been used.

The fruit or vegetables were then colored realistically with a brush

A glass dome

and liquid. This required much skill and could only be done by artists. The various objects were then fastened onto a wire and arranged in whatever group it was to fit into.

Wax flowers were commonly used under glass domes. Domes were made by blowing the glass with a tube, making a hollow, rounded cylinder. It was then cut off at the open end, to make the desired height. The domes were set onto a walnut base, deep or shallow, round or oval, resting on three ball feet. It was at the time when black walnut was used quite generally for furnishings in the home. The domes were set into a groove in the base. Some bases were stained black and some were of ebony. An unusual base was one made of pottery to represent a piece of a tree trunk, in color. And still another had a zinc lining. Both of these could have fernery put into them. A red woolen cord was placed around the base of the glass, but most of these have been moth-eaten and thrown away. Some globes were high and slender, other low and squatty. Some were flattened and oval in shape.

My collection of glass domes has some choice pieces, the choicest of which is a basket of wax fruit. The basket is made of reed, standing 12 inches high with a handle. A tall round dome covers it, 20 inches high, on a black base. One side of the basket is turned down, the better to show the fruit. There is an open pea pod, nuts, a bunch of white grapes and one of red grapes, a pear, a cucumber, and a peach. This basket of fruit was the means of my discovering how wax fruit was made.

Glass domes were placed over many ornamental vases of wax flowers, of cloth flowers, and even of spun glass ornaments. It was a most popular fad to have stuffed birds on branches in realistic poses under the domes. Besides these, a vase of the deceased person's hair would be set up for funerals.

The material for wax flowers could be purchased in a box, complete. Once, when invited to buy in a New Hampshire home, I found such a box on a shelf in a closet. In it were sheets of wax, wire, cloth ribbon, cloth leaves, and a tool. At the time, I was interested only in primitives of wood, iron, and tin. I laid the box back and have regretted my decision over the years.

The sheets of colored wax were shaped into flowers, petals, and buds. This was done with the tool and each flower was made of its appropriate color. The wire stem was wound with the green waxy ribbon and the flower was fastened at the end. Buds and leaves were fastened in their proper places. The worker knew the exact details of every part of the bouquet. Cloth, too, was colored, calico was used, and cut into realistic shapes to represent a spray of flowers.

These sprays were placed in early glass vases or in Staffordshire china vases. The floor of the base standard often had a covering; one in my collection was purple velvet. On the under part of the base is a label of the maker, stating the fact that he supplied such decorations for funerals, purple being the sign of mourning.

One of the greatest feats was making ornaments of spun glass and placing them under a dome. Ships of the sea, flying the stars and stripes; birds in nests, sitting on eggs; birds flying, with long plumage; birds on branches, these were all fastened to a fine coil wire, which caused the birds and other objects to quiver with any motion. Even the colors were those of Nature.

Among my several glass dome ornaments is one that came from Switzerland. It is a miniature Swiss village on a marble base, resting on three ball feet. It has houses and a church of cardboard, miniature trees, and a pond made with a small mirror.

Rare clocks were put under glass domes, instead of being placed in a regular case. A friend has a full-rigged ship on painted waves under a long dome. Beneath is a music box, and when the music is started the ship rocks on the ocean in realistic manner. Glass domes were made in all sizes from the tiny ones to such as covered the musical ship.

Although few of us still prize shadow boxes or glass dome ornaments, many museums have them, preserved for posterity so that our generations might learn the arts of the past.

34

MUSICAL GLASSES

DO YOU REMEMBER WHEN DADDY OR BIG BROTHER MADE MUSIC AT THE table by filling tumblers with water and then tapping them lightly with a spoon? Each tumbler had a different amount of water in it to make a different vibration or pitch. If two were struck at the same time, the two tones made a chord.

A still more thrilling feat was to make music by moistening a finger in water and rubbing it around the edge of the tumbler. That made a beautiful tone.

I little thought that those musical glasses of my childhood would come back into my life again. Up in a beautiful 19th century house in New Ipswich, New Hampshire, now owned by the Society of the Preservation of New England Antiquities, is a set of Musical Glasses. They are in a deep, square-box holder, lined with felt, measuring about thirty inches square and ten inches deep. The glasses are shaped like goblets of various sizes, their stems set down into the holder. There are twenty-four of them, all pitched according to their size, in three octaves running from middle C. Sharps and flats are included. Each goblet has its pitch stamped on it in gold and black. At the side of the box is a small shelf that pulls out. This is at the front corner and holds the bowl of water that is needed to play on the glasses.

With the set of glasses, a book of directions is included. It notes the year of 1830 and says the cost was from 40 to 75 dollars. The book has the name of the company on the front cover:

Grand Harmonican
Francis H. Smith
Sole Patentee
Baltimore

The directions state that the glasses were played with two hands. The ball of the middle finger was moistened in the water, then rubbed gently around the edge of the glass. The hand was in a flat position. The thumb was used to dampen the tone before the next one was made. The tune was played by using the middle finger of each hand, changing as desired, and either thumb could be used to dampen the vibration. Because the scale included flats and sharps, many tunes could be played in several keys.

Musical glasses

Turning to Chambers's Encyclopedia, I found that such a musical instrument was called a harmonica and was invented by Benjamin Franklin. He was in London in 1760 and there saw performances with musical glasses. He regulated his glasses by the size, which gave the pitch. It took several years for him to perfect his invention.

In the 17th century, a similar instrument had been made. In 1746 and again in 1750, performances had been given by using water in the glasses for pitch. Mozart and Beethoven had written music for such an instrument. It was said that the nerves at the end of the finger were greatly affected by the friction of rubbing the goblet edge and after a performance of any great length, the player fainted. The instrument was in vogue for some time.

Today, one sees an occasional performance on these musical glasses. But the popularity of musical bells, bells made with graded pitch, has usurped the place of glasses. The case of twenty-four musical glasses up in New Ipswich is one more pastime of the earlier days to be cherished.

35

WHEN FANS WERE IN FAVOR

WHEN PLANNING FOR SOCIAL EVENTS, THE WOMEN FOLK ALWAYS BE-
gin by thinking of costumes and related accessories. And in the Gay Nineties an important dress accessory for any occasion of consequence was the
fan. Many were the varieties of fans, all examples of beautiful handwork.

Fans go far back in history to the Assyrians, Egyptians, and Greeks
of the warm climates. In those days fans were large and leaf-shaped,
carried on the ends of poles. They played an important role both in the
homes and in religious ceremonies. Female slaves and boys carried them
to keep the air in circulation and to keep the flies from both people and
food. In the church, they were also used to keep the air in circulation and
to keep the flies from the sacred vessels and cloths. Fans of peacock
feathers were used by the pope's attendants in solemn processions.

The folding fans are best known. They are said to have been created
by the Japanese, who based their creation on the idea of the folding wings
of the bat. Fans were made of parchment, satin, crepe, or tulle and folded
in 12 to 24 equal parts. The sticks were wood, ivory, metal, or mother-
of-pearl. The leaf, made of two equal pieces, was plain with lace trims,
embroidered or painted with colored scenes. Some were works of art,
fashioned by goldsmiths, carvers, and jewelers and painted by reputable
artists.

We have three fans in our family. One was a gift to me for my high
school graduation. I remember carrying it on a long chain of imitation
pearls. Mother's graduation fan has sandalwood sticks, studded with
sequins. It is satin with feather trimming across the top edge. A third
fan has ivory sticks beautifully carved. It is of satin with rose point lace
appliquéd in a design across the leaf and it has a lace edge. There are
many collectors of fans and I have seen them displayed in glass, fan-
shaped frames.

When fans were in favor

At an auction one summer I saw a folding fan, which was sold in a lot with other fans. It was red like the one we had years ago. It shut up into box-like sides and the ends were hooked with a wire loop. You opened it by turning it inside out.

Another type of fan we had was worked with a silk cord. It was a red tube. You pulled a cord at one end and out came a plaited, round fan. You pulled a cord at the other end and the fan folded back into place, in its case. I remember how we children used to play with it. No doubt we wore it out. Both of these fans were smaller than the kind with sticks and a leaf. Collectors are looking for such fans, the folding type, both red and black.

The days of beautiful fans are over. We use palm leaf fans to cool ourselves in summertime and we often carry a small "dinner" fan to a functional dinner or to a public gathering. Perhaps well-ventilated and air-conditioned halls and auditoriums have something to do with the disappearance of those beautiful fans.

Now a report from London tells of the revival of the fan, a "delightfully feminine accessory." Fashionable women are seen carrying them to cocktail parties, receptions, dances, and to the theater. Fans are staging a comeback, as all styles do, completing a cycle of a number of years. Those who own such heirlooms will rejoice in their possessions.

36

IN THE GAY NINETIES THE STEREOSCOPE

THERE WAS NO CINERAMA, THE THREE-DIMENSION MOVING PICTURE, IN the Gay Nineties. In those years the stereoscope held sway. Families still cherish their stereoscope and their neatly tied stacks of stereoscopic pictures. You'll find them tied with a cord or an old ribbon, tucked away in the drawer of an old secretary or a highboy. You'll find them there if some collector has not beguiled the owners into parting with them!

In the heyday of the pictures, there were various holders in which the views were kept, made of black walnut on the jigsaw. One had two sections the size of the picture, with a partition between. Another had three narrow shelves slanting to either side of the center upright. These were kept on the parlor table or on a what-not shelf, right handy so they could be used, especially when entertaining company. Today, those black walnut holders are perfect for letters or envelopes, standing on an old desk. At auctions, the bidding is sharp for them, showing how old things can be put to use in modern ways.

An Englishman invented the stereoscope in 1838. The idea was to have two of the same picture, one for each eye, seen through two separate magnifying lenses. This gave a third dimension. It has been recorded that Oliver Wendell Holmes designed the frame that held the pictures. This had a long, slender arm with a short handle at right angles, and another arm on which were wires that held the picture, which could be moved nearer to or farther from the lenses. The lenses were set into a cup-shape paper or cloth frame that was held against the eyes. This was attached to the long arm with the handle.

A decade after the Civil War, the stereoscope became very popular. Photographers sprung up in many localities, here and across the water, taking pictures of scenic spots, famous people, and family groups. A friend who was ill in bed used to say she traveled in Rome one day, in

In the gay nineties the stereoscope

France another day, and in scenic America still another. The pictures were not only entertaining but educational.

In our collection of pictures are some that show the flood in Worcester, March 30, 1876. A Worcester photographer took eighteen views of the destruction caused by the flood, centering at the South end. Another set of pictures shows the Johnstown flood, May 31, 1889. And a Northampton photographer took the views of the Mill River Valley Great Flood of May 6, 1874.

Family group pictures taken on Martha's Vineyard and in Falmouth about 1875 show some of my relatives on a vacation, and one at the time of the visit of President McKinley when cottages were gaily trimmed with bunting and flags. Any group could hire a photographer and have stereoscopic pictures made.

A French mounting was quite different and very fascinating. The picture was made of two sheets placed together and when viewed in a holder, color appeared and pin-point lights showed up as lights in chandeliers or as candles. These French pictures today are much sought after by collectors.

The intense interest in the three-dimensional pictures brought out many inventions. Several types of pictures and arrangements to hold them appeared in this country and across the water, some of them of large dimensions. One was called the stereographoscope. This was used for the French double-sheet pictures and the pin-point lights made most unusual scenes.

Stereoscopic pictures cannot be mentioned without bringing to mind the magic lantern. That was another very popular pastime for the entire family. The lantern was made of tin in the shape of a chimney. A bull's eye of glass was at the front end and a kerosene lamp was at the back.

A colored glass picture slide was put into a slot and drawn through to move one scene on to another. The pictures were made in a series of motions, of some amusing caricature doing something which moved along and made a story. A large sheet was pinned up at one end of the room and the lantern was placed on a table at a proper distance. It made a happy evening for the family when company dropped in. Many lanterns and pictures are still to be found, not entirely lost to posterity.

Today's Cinerama has taken the same principle that was born with the stereoscope. Of course they are not to be compared with each other, for each generation has its new inventions. The pleasure afforded by the stereoscope and the magic lantern filled its purpose in those early days.

37

WHEN THERE'S A LIGHT IN THE WINDOW

IN THE GAS-LIGHT ERA, FATHER AND MOTHER HAD A BEAUTIFUL CRAN-berry red glass shade on the gas-light in the front hall. It was on the newell post at the foot of the stairs, and with the small gas flame it gave out a very dim light. Today, that same fluted red shade with its delicately etched pattern tops a clear glass lamp, standing on my grand piano near the bay window of the music room. With a strong electric bulb, a beautiful red glow is cast over the room and out the window to the street.

A friend once remarked, "I love to see your red light as I pass. When I see lights in the window, I always try to imagine who the people are that live in the house and what they are doing. Lights from colorful lamps are so friendly!"

Always has a light sent out its glow. In the old country, the early fireplaces were built with a window at the back so the fire on the hearth might send out its light into the night. Passersby would see the light and would come to the door, asking to share the warmth of the fire and the hospitality of the family.

In the new country, such fireplaces have been built and the same spirit of sharing the warmth of the fire has gone forth with the light through the window.

Shall we ever forget the story of Polly Pepper! Brought up in poverty, she scrimped and toiled with a longing in her heart for much that she never had. She bent over her sewing with a lone candle for a light. She said she would have one thing when she was rich—she would have a lighted candle in every room in the house, at every window. That to her would be the greatest joy imaginable; sharing her happiness with all the passersby.

On the coast of New England, many a wife has set a light in the window, sending out a welcome across the waves. This light showed that a loved one was on the ocean and a wife was at home waiting for his re-

There's a light in the window

turn. A story has long been told of a lone widow who could not believe that her husband had been lost in a shipwreck. Every night she set her lighted lamp in the window to show she was waiting. This she did until she passed away, always with the belief that her feeble light could be seen out to sea.

I'll never forget the time I saw a welcome light shining in a little farm house up in New Hampshire. A friend and I had driven up to spend the day with an antiques enthusiast. When we started for home, he directed us through a cross-cut that would save us about ten miles. It was a wooded, dirt road but we thought nothing of it until the inky blackness began to bear down upon us. We drove without speaking, literally scared stiff, fearful that the road might not take us out to the main highway. All of a sudden, through the trees, we spied a faint light in a distant farm house. We let out a sigh of relief, for we knew the light meant habitation and protection.

Today sees lamps of all descriptions salvaged from the past, electrified and given another lease on life. The old lamps have become so popular that they are sought out at auctions and in shops, where they bring fabulous prices. One particular lamp with a globe base and a globe shade in color has taken the name of *Gone With the Wind* because such a lamp was used in the moving picture.

The tall piano lamp, the table lamp of brass or nickel, the hanging diningroom lamp that traveled up and down on chains and wheels, and even the common glass lamp with a reflector at the back that shed its feeble rays out in the kitchen have all been put to use once more, with electricity. And as we pass down the street, we see their light in the windows and we think of the hospitality they are sending out into the night.

38

THE GHOSTS OF THE LAMPLIGHTERS

INTO OUR NEIGHBORHOOD, LIKE IN ALL OTHER NEIGHBORHOODS IN THE city, there came, long ago, a man to check and adjust the city gas lights. He came with his ladder over his shoulder, one arm thrust between two rungs, walking all day on his rounds.

He was a cheerful person, very attentive to business but ready to chat with anyone who stopped. He had been on his job thirty odd years, beginning as a little boy, going on the rounds with an older man. This man had a full gray beard and he came in an old Ford wagon, rattling along the street. The wagons had curtains that were rolled up and tied in fair weather and dropped in stormy weather. The ladder hung on hooks at one side and a lantern was ready to use when dusk came, quite necessary when the street light had to be tinkered with. The jolly, bearded man brought along the little boy, eager to be of any assistance but delighted to ride around and watch the process each evening.

Then one day, the old Ford wagon did not appear. In its place came the little boy, now a grown man, with the ladder over his shoulder. He was then stocky in build and for this reason, he admitted, he trudged along on his feet that he might become slim and more comfortable. He had taken over the job with the passing of the old man.

Street lighting has been a law for many centuries. In New York, city lamps were ordered in December 1697, "in the dark of the moon, for the ease of the inhabitants." Every seventh house had a lantern—called "lanthorn" because the windows were of thin sheets of horn—hung out on a pole. The expense was shared by the seven neighbors who benefited by it. These lanterns were attended by a watch, who would call out, "Lanthorn and a whole candle light! Hang out your lights here!"

Candles changed to oil lamps and oil lamps became gas lights, illuminated by a torch. The lantern changed in shape. There were four sides, tapered at the bottom with a tapered top part that had a vent for air.

144

The ghost of the lamplighters

A door opened at the front side. This lantern was fastened to a post, a sturdy wooden post at first and then an iron post, always with two arms at the top on which the ladder could rest.

Robert Louis Stevenson, in 1850, caught the excitement attending the coming of the lamplighter:

> My tea is nearly ready and the sun has left the sky,
> It's time to take the window to see Leerie going by.
> For every night at tea-time and before you take your seat,
> With lantern and with ladder, he comes posting up the street.
> . . . .
> For we are very lucky, with a lamp before our door,
> And Leerie stops to light it as he lights as many more.

All of this romance our generations have lost—this leisurely lighting of the street lights! Then came a gas light, lighted from the main source, placed among the bright electric lights. Many old homes and those copied from the old style architecture have lamp posts out front. Trying to capture that lost romance! Not with candle and not with an oil lamp, but with an electric bulb, lighted from within doors. And none of those lamp posts have the arms on which rested the ladder.

The old lamplighter with his lantern and his ladder has passed. But for many there are the memories of his trudging up the street, climbing his ladder, lighting the lamp and off again for others. Perhaps his ghost follows the men of today who carry on.

39

BULL'S EYE PANES AND PICTURE WINDOWS

ON THE EDGE OF WORCESTER IS AN OLD BRICK HOUSE, NOW YELLOW BUT once natural brick. It has stood as a landmark for over a century. One day, I saw carpenters breaking down the windows, one in the front room and one in the second room. Soon, in the course of time, I saw picture windows.

Up in Oakham, the home of my father's childhood, there is an old house at the top of the hill that has stood there for much more than a century. A second generation of the family added a small bay window on each side of the front door, on the first floor. A short time ago, as I passed through the town, I was amazed to see that carpenters had dismantled the bays and put in picture windows. Another old house changed to meet the modern whims!

Windows have been very expressive in the progress of living. Man's first homes had no windows. At the time of the Romans, the well-to-do families used horn or shell or mica to cover their window openings. The poorer class resorted to animal skins, shorn of their hair, and oiled paper, for as long as 1,000 years. In Venice and Genoa, where glass was made, glass windows appeared in the 12th and 13th centuries, but the panes were so rare up until the 16th century that a family took them when they moved.

In England, glass windows were taxed beginning in 1696 and no house could have more than ten windows without a payment of 4 shillings a window. People bricked up the openings and when they built a new house they counted their windows up to 9. This went on until 1845. The houses were dark and dismal, and the light and air was not considered a part of healthful living.

When the Pilgrims came to this country, their frame houses had oiled skins or oiled paper covering the few window openings. The windows were set high to make for more seclusion, from trespassers and any attacks from the Indians. Writing back to England, the new settlers asked the families that planned to come over to bring glass for their windows. Because of the scarcity of glass, the panes were small and diamond-shaped, six by four inches. These were set in casement windows that opened outwards.

Bull's eye panes

By 1700, larger panes of glass were available and sash windows were made, an improvement over casement windows. At first there were three frames in a window, then there were two. Remember when we raised one of those small windows, how it shivered up the sides and we fastened it with a snap catch? Weights and cords were not long in following. The panes were oblong and the glass was wavy and mottled. The division of the number of panes was uneven; nine in the upper and twelve in the lower, or six in the upper and nine in the lower. Occasionally, the upper sash had more panes than the lower, but not as a common thing.

The first process of making glass was to blow it onto a flat surface and roll it out with a rolling pin. Where the tube had left the hot mixture in the center, there would be a lump, or as it was called a "bull's eye." The smooth, perfect part of the square was cut into diamond-shaped pieces and the bull's eye was called waste. Another generation used those bull's eyes in doorways, across the top and down the sides. They were even put in cellar windows.

The history of windows and glass, that of the old country and in this country, covers many interesting chapters. Perhaps no change in the mode of living shows more than in the progress from skins and oiled paper, or even horn, to the large picture windows of the 20th century. It would seem a vital question of health, with air and sunshine considered, to have many window openings with picture windows for extra attraction.

40

EVEN DOORS HAVE A HISTORY

YOU WOULD NEVER THINK THAT A DOOR—A COMMON DOOR THAT YOU open or close, that you bump into, that you slam when you are angry and have to go back and close it quietly—you would never think that a door has a history.

In the beginning, the doorway to the huts and tents had merely a mat of straw, skin, or cloth. As man perfected his ways of living, so came houses with windows and doors.

When there was need of protection against the Indians and other marauders, the front door of the first two-room house was large and heavy. It was called a batten door because it had battens or small strips nailed on the outside. These strips were studded with heavy nails. The inside part was made of several boards placed horizontally, held in place by the vertical batten strips on the outside. Heavy iron hinges held the door to the heavy oak jamb. A wooden latch was often used and the door was barricaded with a heavy wooden bar that dropped into a wooden holder. This was all for protection in those uncertain days.

Inside doors between the rooms were panelled doors, with iron latches that had a thumb press. It is said that Paul Revere made iron latches, hinges, and door knockers. Those first hinges were called H and L because the two parts took the shape of these two letters.

When the houses were built with more rooms, two or three stories high, the front doors were made with panels. The frame around the four panels made a cross and that around six panels made a double cross. Those were the days when witchcraft was running rampant. Anything with a cross or a hex mark was believed to protect the owner from being subject to the evil spirits. These crosses made what is called today a "Christian" door.

Later 18th-century houses of the Georgian type have doors that match the front door on either side of the house. It was in such a house that

Even doors have a history

bull's eye glass was set into frames above the door to let in light from the outside. Perhaps with more artistic beauty, are the windows above a doorway that were made in the shape of a fan. The frame held panes of glass set in a semicircular shape or wooden slats that were set to represent a folding fan.

With no way of attracting attention when standing at the outside door, it was but natural that a door knocker would be created. Knockers of iron were most elaborate, made in the forms of animal heads or other figures. Names of the owners of the house were often inscribed on the lower part of the knocker. Brass followed those of iron. The knocker was bolted through the door to the inside.

In houses of less grandeur, a thinner panel door was at the front. This had an iron latch with a thumb press. Some could be opened only from the inside, which made for protection. This brought about the latch string and the nursery rhyme that followed. A short leather thong was tied to the handle of the latch, a hole was cut through the door above it, and the thong was thrust through the hole and hung outside. There it hung for anyone to pull. It lifted the latch inside and then the door opened. If anyone wanted privacy, the latch string was pulled in and no one could enter.

> "Cross patch, draw the latch,
> Sit before the fire and spin;
> Take a cup, drink it up
> And call your neighbors in."

Or again:

> "Knock at the door, peep in,
> Draw the latch and walk in."

In the days when swine and geese wandered through the streets, a door that divided into two sections was found necessary. This was common in the towns where the Dutch had settled and thus came the name of Dutch door. The upper half could be opened while the lower remained closed, thus keeping out any wandering barnyard animals or birds. Although designed for an outside use, many bars in a tavern had such a door, with a narrow shelf put onto the lower half, on which mugs of beer or other drinks could be laid for guests to take.

One more door recently came to my attention. It is a strange one and not commonly known.

Services for the dead were held in the home, at the time of the 17th and 18th centuries. They were held in the front room, the parlor. Because of the size of the coffin, a door had been made in the outside wall, leading to the side yard. Through this the coffin could be carried. This was called a "coffin door," and at no other time was it used, except at a funeral.

In the Gay Nineties, the front door changed from a single door to a double door. These had glass set into the upper part, as much as half with glass. Sometimes, only two small windows were set into the upper part. Glass allowed light to enter the hallways and it also enabled those on the inside to look out and see who wanted to come in. The doors were made of beautiful wood with more or less fancy design. The knocker gave way to a bell, first the one that was hung on a coil of wire inside the door, which jangled when the outside knob was pulled and later when electric wires were run to a bell hanging on the kitchen wall. Some early bells were on the inside of the door and a crank outside made them ring. Hardware changed from that of ironware to brass. Inside doors had knobs of glass as well as brass. Even silver lustre and white ironstone was used. In the time of the height of the Sandwich factory, knobs were often made like floral paper weights.

Folding doors became popular in the Gay Nineties. The doors slid between the wall or folded in the middle before sliding. Such doors were very convenient, partly or wholly closed, for those were the days of furnace heat which was never entirely adequate for the large rooms and high ceilings.

A hinge which apparently has no name is found in some old houses. An ordinary hinge is made in two parts, each one setting into the other, on a flat horizontal edge. If that edge was made on a slant, the door does not remain stationary, but swings back to a closed position. The lower hinge is not put directly under the upper, but a little more inside the jamb. If you open the door and pass through, you will find that the door closes behind you. That is caused by the weight of the door on a slanting hinge. One such door is in a bedroom in Governor Gore's brick mansion in Waltham, Massachusetts. Five such doors are in an old house not far from Worcester. They lead from the hallway by the front door, into the parlor and into the living room. After you enter either side, the door closes behind you. This doubtless was to keep out the cold that came from the open hallway that led up to the third floor.

Today's doors inside and outside are severely plain, made of one panel of reinforced wood. Inside doors rest on the floor with no threshhold. All of this is for the purpose of saving labor, with no panels and framework of moldings to catch the dust.

As I pass beautiful doorways on old houses, I often think what pleasure can be derived from studying them. They speak of the age of the house and of the man who built it. Many are the collectors who photograph old doors and doorways. I have heard the family tell the story of a stranger who saw a beautiful door and stopped to admire it. He knocked and said to the owner who came to answer his summons, "I like your door and would like to buy it." The answer for him was, "We like it, too."

Even doors have a history.

PART III
IN MILADY'S CHAMBER

41

THE DAY OF THE SPINSTERS IS GONE

IT WAS WITH FEAR THAT A YOUNG WOMAN IN COLONIAL DAYS LOOKED ahead and saw her chances of getting married grow dim. Marriage came early then. As her sisters and friends found their perfect mate, she realized her fate hung in the balance if she did not marry. But nothing could be done about it.

A lover brought gifts of a strange assortment—a wooden feather bed smoother, a broad wooden dress stay called a busk, both of which had initials cut into them. Perhaps he also brought a pie crimper used when pinking pies and sundry carved tools for the pantry. Two things were synonymous with his wooing; the courting lamp and a courting mirror. The lamp was what the lovers used when sitting together in the front room. It was a small glass lamp holding scarcely enough whale oil to burn through a short evening. The courting mirror was a beautiful thing, carried in a box. It was about a foot long and eight inches wide, with a narrow border of inlay and an ornamental top. If and when the lover brought this mirror, he came to declare his love. If she returned the mirror to the box, it was a sign that she was rejecting him. As wedding gifts, the maiden was given more things for her new home, omens of happiness and health. A long-handled fry pan, a splintered birch broom, a wafer iron, and a waffle iron were included. And her dowry contained countless linen towels, sheets, and pillow cases which she had made with the help of the family from flax grown on the place.

Little wonder a sister looked on in awe at the preparations of an older sister. She was doomed to be a family drudge, a spinster. She would have to do the spinning, which occupation brought out the word spinster. She would have to be the dressmaker and in fact help in all the chores that fell to the women. The name spinster implied that she had no choice in the matter; she was relegated to the chimney corner.

As the years went by and spinning ceased to be a family occupation,

155

The day of the spinster is gone

the word spinster changed to old maid. That was worse yet; to be unmarried and called an old maid! Chances were she would become an old
maid Aunt, too! She was credited as being petty, small-minded, exacting,
and fussy. "Set" beyond words! Even her dressing was different; prim,
proper. "Old maidish" applied to her manner, too. Nieces and nephews
in the family gave the old maid the title of old maid Aunt. She was supposed to do any and all jobs and she knew how children ought to be
brought up even though she never had any.

There was a play in the Gay Nineties titled *Green Stockings*. It
stemmed from an English custom of an older sister wearing green stockings if a younger sister married. These had to be worn until she found
her man.

As the Gay Nineties with all their customs faded away, so changed
the attitude toward old maids and old maid Aunts. A wholesome change
of attitude took place, subtly but definitely. The unmarried woman became
a Bachelor Girl. This did not in any way lap over into a bachelor's terri-
tory. But it was supposed to show that the girl was free and unfettered
as was an unmarried man. The Bachelor Girl stepped out into a world of
careers and business. She was free to choose and pick her work and her
play. She even left her family and went off to a job and apartment of her
own. She seemed so free after her business hours, she was envied by her
sisters who were carrying on in a home with their family.

Bachelor girls and unmarried women have made a place for themselves. The world could not get along without them.

42

SOAPSTONE SLABS AND WARMING PANS

A TOUCH OF COLD, WINDY WEATHER IS ALWAYS EXPECTED AFTER JAN-
uary comes in. That is when we have to try hard to think that winter is behind us and spring is not too far away. That is the time we are mindful of
the old saying, "As the days begin to lengthen, the cold begins to
strengthen."

We put on our warm clothing when we go out and we push up our
thermostats when we are in. Cold nights follow cold days and whether
it is old-fashioned or not, we resort to our electric pads and our hot water
bottles. Even rubber hot water bottles have been made more attractively.
They are made today so that one side has a raised rubber addition and
the other is plain. The raised rubber part is not as hot as the plain side,
which makes it more comfortable to hold in the beginning.

Aluminum hot water bottles, shaped round and flat, are a blessing
on cold winter nights, because you can pour in very hot water, put on a
flannel cover and toward morning, when the night is still cold, you can
take off the cover and have a warm bottle. Those made of aluminum must
date as far back as the Gay Nineties. I have a tin hot water holder in
my collection, oblong and flat, that goes back farther than those of aluminum. And today, it is the electric blanket—heated by the turn of a
switch.

Some families still cherish the soapstone slab that served past generations. The slabs measure about six by eight inches and are a scant two
inches thick. For more than a century, soapstone slabs have been a boon
on cold days and cold nights. Heated in the oven, a slab was warmed and
would hold the heat for many hours. Slatted frames were made to hold
the slab when it was used as a foot warmer in the house or out in the
sleigh. And when bedtime came, held by its wire handle, it was thrust
between the cold sheets, taking off the chill. An aquisition for my collection is a soapstone slab with the owner's name cut into it; R. D.

Shipley. This is cut in a curve across the top, with a fancy scroll below. Small pieces of soapstone were made to hold in the hands or inside a muff or pocket when going to church or sociables.

In Europe, many a family used bags of warm rye meal as a means of warming a bed, or for a sick patient. Huge pans of meal were warmed in the oven and then poured into small bags made of coarse cotton. Several of these bags made for comfortable sleeping.

Soapstone slabs and warming pans

Any family that has a brass or copper warming pan leaning against the chimney breast today little realizes what it meant to our ancestors to use such an article. It was filled with live embers from the fire, of wood or coal, and thrust between the sheets and moved back and forth to take off the chill. Collectors claim today that the more points the decoration in the cover has, the more monetary value the warming pan has. The points or holes allowed the gasses to escape. Some pans with much decoration have as many as twenty-one holes.

A long-handled warming pan of tin is in my collection. Incidentally, this piece began my collection of tinware. Filled with hot water, it could make a cold bed in a cold room comfortable. It is very thin, round, with a screw cap in the center where the water was poured in. The tubular handle is made in three sections, soldered together. There is a thick-headed, short-handled tin warmer for water. Such warming pans of tin were made in the middle of the 19th century, while those of brass or copper have served the families for close to three centuries.

Foot stoves or foot warmers were made to take in a sleigh, to meeting, to singing school or social gatherings. Those for the sleigh were shaped like a slanting pillow of tin, covered with ingrain carpeting. One burned cakes of charcoal and the other used hot water. That one was made of copper. The tin one has a large star in the handle and smaller ones around both ends. A star stood for religion.

Spring is supposed to be just around the corner when January thaws hold forth. As more storms blow down upon us and the days begin to lengthen, we scoff at the biting cold and resort to any and all warming aids.

43

THE STORY OF BANDBOXES

IN MY SEARCH FOR WOODENWARE, I HAVE BEEN INVITED INTO MANY homes. It has been a common occurrence to go into kitchens and pantries and then go up into the attic and even down to the cellar.

One day in the attic of a house, I chanced upon several things that interested me. A sawbuck table for my museum, lustre chinaware and a large bandbox stuffed with odds and ends. Down in the cellar was a rare oaken bucket with a trap door which I added to my purchases.

The bandbox seemed hopelessly battered. It was cardboard—sides, top and bottom—and covered with wallpaper depicting some scene. That night, I stuffed it, putting it into shape; and I flattened the cover with heavy blocks. In the morning, I found I had a perfect bandbox with no breaks. It had a picture of the opening of the Erie Canal on the sides and on the cover was the ship *Constitution,* flying the American flag, in color. On it were the letters GRAND CANAL and around the rim of the cover was "Prosperity to Our Commerce and Manufacturers." I straightway went to the Public Library and found the record of the Grand Erie Canal's opening, October 2, 1824. I knew I had a rare bandbox.

A collector soon heard of my find and came to buy the bandbox, including the history I had found. Even though I was collecting woodenware, I missed the bandbox from the top of our highboy. So it was not long before I found another one to take its place. This one has a conventional pattern with a foreign scene. Someone then gave me a wooden meal box covered with wall paper and then I bought a medium-sized bandbox made of cardboard.

A tiny bandbox, scarcely five inches long, bought at an auction was something to awaken my real interest. It was all cardboard, covered with wallpaper of no particular pattern. The cover and bottom were sewed to the rim and sides with fine stitches of coarse thread. I was told that the little box stood on a small table by the side of a bed and was used to hold the lacey nightcap of the grandmother. It seemed to express so much to me!

From the family encyclopedia comes the description of a bandbox. "The two small strips of linen worn at the neck as part of legal, clerical and academic dress are known as 'bands.' They are the survival of the falling collar of the 17th century. The light cardboard boxes now used to carry millinery were formerly made to carry neckbands; hence the name 'bandbox!'"

The name Hannah Davis has become synonomous with bandboxes. She was born in East Jaffery, New Hampshire, or possibly over the boundary in Rindge, in 1784. She lived a span of 79 years. Her father was Peter Davis, a skilled maker of wooden clocks and cheese boxes. He taught his daughter much lore about trees and wood. When Hannah conceived the idea of making bandboxes, she directed the cutting of the trees, which were old spruce trees. She began making boxes of thin veneer; the first pieces of the trunk for smaller boxes and the center for larger boxes. Hannah designed the machine that sliced the wood. The sides of the box were bent to an oval shape and nailed while the wood was green. The bottoms and tops were made of old pine, the sides nailed to the rims.

Old newspapers were used to line the boxes and block-print wallpaper was used to cover them. The patterns of the wallpaper were gay, depicting scenes, events, canal boats, ships, railways, capitols, schools and many public buildings. Because the bandboxes were soon used in stage-coach traveling, many places and buildings seen on such trips were used in decoration.

Wallpaper appeared in this country about 1725, ordered from Lon-

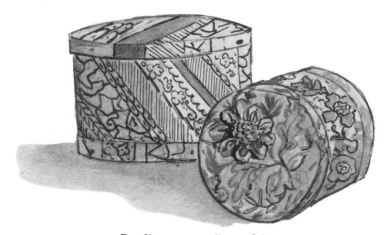

Bandboxes are collectors' items

don or Paris. It was not generally used until the beginning of the 19th century. Some wallpaper was made especially for bandboxes, but more often is was cut from sheets and then from rolls coming in long lengths. The favorite color for the background was a soft shade of blue, but green, yellow, and tan were also used. Much brown was used in the designs.

Hannah Davis soon made her bandboxes of cardboard, with wooden tops and bottoms, nailed to the rims and sides. A label appears on the inside of the cover in the genuine boxes made by Hannah Davis. This reads:

Warrented Nailed
Bandboxes
Manufactured by
Hannah Davis
East Rindge, N.H.

At first Hannah Davis used her boxes in barter for supplies for her home. Then when she had accumulated enough to sell, she set out in a wagon of a prairie schooner type and headed for factory towns: Manchester, New Hampshire, and Lowell, Massachusetts. Here she sold the boxes for 25 and 50 cents to young women from the best families who carried the latest fashion idea back to their home towns.

Many of the boxes were made in nests, graded in several sizes. Used for traveling, they held collars, caps, hats, and millinery. Bonnets were the large collapsible pumpkin hoods that could be thrown back. Because stage-coach travelers could carry only 28 pounds of baggage, the lightweight bandbox was an advantage over the heavy wooden trunks covered with calf skins that appeared later. The first wooden holder was called a "trunk" because it was made from a tree trunk. Cut a proper length and hollowed, a section was taken off for a cover and hinged with wire hinges, the opposite side was flattened for the bottom. Although heavy and awkward, it made a very usable holder.

Several Manufactures of bandboxes appeared in the nineteenth century—H. Barnes, Manufacturer of Philadelphia; Barnard Andrews of New York; Thomas Day, Jr. of New York; and Putnam and Hoff of Hartford, Connecticut, who advertised paper hanging as well as making bandboxes. One bandbox has this name of a manufacturer with his address on a label:

From
S. M. Hurlbert's
Paste Board, Band Box and Paper Hangings

Manufactory
No. 25. Court Street
Boston

Such a label shows that wall papers and pasteboard used to make bandboxes were sold at a manufacturing place. Bandboxes did not appear until
the 19th century. Since they were lined with newspapers; their date of
manufacture can be approximated. One of mine is dated 1841, 1842, and
1843.

"He looks as if he had stepped out of a bandbox" is often said today.
Bandboxes make a fascinating addition to a collector's home.

44

NEEDLES AND PINS ARE IMPORTANT

Needles and pins, needles and pins,
When a man marries, his trouble begins.

THAT JINGLE IS "AS OLD AS THE HILLS!" BUT OLDER YET ARE NEEDLES
and pins. In pre-historic time, needles were of bone, ivory, wood, bronze,
metal and even of thorns. Savages must have sewed their garments, because those primitive implements have been unearthed. The sewing needle
is claimed to be one of the oldest implements of man.

Pins, too, were made by prehistoric man, of materials at hand: thorns
and small bones of fish. Some have been found of bronze, copper, and iron.
Pins were made with ornamental heads of gold. Both needles and pins
were three and four inches in length.

So it seems as if man has always sewed and pinned. Today's generations point with pride to the old samplers, quilts, undergarments, and the
dated and initialed homespun sheets and blankets. Every child had to
learn to use a needle and thimble at a very young age, as those samplers
testify—the child's age was worked in one corner. This stint work fell to
my Mother. To lessen the tediousness, my Mother began at the top step
in the flight of stairs and slid down one step and then another as the sewing
progressed. She began at the age of three.

When I was learning to sew, at the early age of five as a little cotton
bag testifies, I was much impressed by a story that I was told. A young
man became interested in two sisters and he could not decide which one
he wanted to marry. He said he would take the one as his wife who could
sew a seam the quicker of the two. As he was threading the two needles,
he decided which sister he wanted. So he gave her a short thread and the
other sister a long thread. The sister with the shorter thread did her seam
in quicker time. The moral pointed out to me as I progressed in my sewing
was to use a short thread!

Needles and pins are found in history

When we children were little we played a game of sewing. We sat in a row, each with the hem of our dress in our hands. The teacher stood in front, chanting:

> "I'll give you so much work to do,
> Needle, thread and thimble, too.
> If you don't get it done by the time I get back,
> I'll lay the stick across your back.
>
> I'm going to Martha Washington's to buy a cup of tea,
> Three loaves of gingerbread, and don't you follow me."

Of course we followed and mocked her as she ordered her tea and gingerbread. Then she chased us back. We held out our dress hems for her to test, holding them taut, while she whacked them with a stick. The one who could not hold the hem taut was "it" next time.

We have all said:

> "See a pin, pick it up.
> All the day, you'll have good luck.
> See a pin, let it lay,
> You'll have bad luck all the day."

How often we are on "pins and needles! Wondering what was going to happen and fearful it might be disturbing! Needles and pins figure in our lives more than we realize. They are rather important things!

An interesting thing to note is that the Shakers were not allowed to cross their knees. The women had a set of two steps on which they rested their foot when they raised their knee to hold their work when sewing. Sometimes a small drawer was in the lower step, to hold any sewing helps. The steps were smaller than those used in climbing to reach.

45

MILADY'S ORNAMENTS

Heigh-ho to Banbury Cross,
To see a fine lady on a white horse;
With rings on her fingers and bells on her toes,
She shall make music wherever she goes.

ALWAYS HAS MANKIND LOVED ORNAMENTS. MEN AS WELL AS WOMEN wore beads, rings, and bracelets. In certain tribes, a certain amount of adornment had a special significance.

The Puritans who came to these shores were a chaste and pious lot. There was little in the way of adornment and all frivolous dressing was condemned. The men wore gold or silver sleeve-buttons and a few women had bracelets and lockets. Plain living was the rule until more wealth came to the colonies when dress and entertainment became more elaborate.

By the end of the eighteenth century, hairwork had become popular. Human hair was used in rings, bracelets, brooches, lockets, watch-chains, charms, and scarf pins. The colors of hair ranged from shades of brown, black and gold to grey. It was taken from living persons as well as from those deceased.

An acquaintance tells me her grandfather was a manufacturer of hair jewelry in Cambridge, Massachusetts. He was the last to carry on jewelry making. Each hair that was used had to be sorted, washed, counted, and tied together. The women of the family did that work. Research shows there was a stool that had a cushion top with a hole in it. A circular pattern with numbers was placed on the cushion. Each hair was fastened to a bobbin, lying over the numbers on the pattern. The bobbins were numbered as they rested on the pattern. The tied ends of the hair were held by a weight down through the hole in the center. As one bobbin after another was thrown over the specific number of strands the pattern called for, the weaving made a hollow tube which traveled down the hole. As the work progressed, the tubular strand was pulled down by a weight. The

167

ends were tied, and then the strand was boiled in water five minutes and dried in the oven.

These tubular strands were then braided and made into bracelets, pins, earrings, and necklaces. After the work was finished and the braid cut off, the ends were shellacked to hold the hair. Beautiful jewelry was made, with a combination of hair and gold.

Another way of making jewelry was to place chopped hair or short ends in a holder of gold, with glass set over it. Rings, brooches, lockets, and watch charms were made in this manner.

Milady's ornaments

A peculiar custom that prevailed among the Colonies was to give mourning rings at the time of a funeral. Made of gold, they represented some form of death such as a skull, cross-bones, a coffin, a serpent, or death's head. Sometimes, the deceased's hair was worked into it. Jewelers had these rings all ready to sell, adding a bit of the deceased's hair, the initials and dates of birth and death.

The custom of giving rings at a funeral, along with gloves and scarfs, prevailed for many years. Everyone who attended had a ring given to him and even those who lived at a distance had rings sent to them. At one funeral in 1738, two hundred rings were given away. The expense was very great. Diaries show that these rings were left in wills, often as many as a tankard full.

Today's generations are wearing jewelry of rare gems which are either heirlooms or purchased for their beauty. Imitations of old jewelry are being made, but no one would resurrect the custom of using hair in jewelry.

46

OLD PIECE BOXES AND SUCH

TIME WAS WHEN THERE WERE STOREROOMS, BIG CLOSETS, "TOP SHELVES," and chests without number. Today, it is an "unfinished attic" and a "play room in the basement." In the days of our grandmothers, what with all those places to store in, nothing was thrown away. Everything came into use at some time or later, and down the generations it was an inborn trait to save. And save they did!

I am the fourth generation that I hear tell about that had the Yankee trait of saving. Father built our house in 1878 when he married Mother, and our family has never moved. I often wish we had moved at least once and then we would have had to do some weeding out in the process. But I really should be grateful for all the piece boxes and such to which I can go any time I am in need of a piece of this and a piece of that.

I well remember the button box with its sliding cover that held fancy buttons; it was kept in a drawer. Pearl buttons, china buttons— probably some of them were Sandwich glass!—and metal buttons with pictures. How a button collector would have gloried in such a box today! Well do I remember being given the button box on a rainy day, having the contents spread out on a newspaper, and playing with them. There was a button bag that held the common buttons. It was made of a piece of calico and was always kept hanging in a closet. That held the buttons needed for daily missing buttons. The wooden button box was what interested me.

There is a box of feathers still carefully packed in newspapers in our storeroom. "Go bring down the box of feathers and see if we haven't got something we can use." That started out the fall of the year as far back as I can remember, whenever a new hat was planned—one made over from whatever happened to be in the hat boxes and the feather box. Ostrich feathers, colored feathers, breasts, and wings made feather ornaments—all waiting to be used some day. Once they adorned hats of velvet,

169

Old pieces boxes and such

plush, and silk beaver. Those old feathers had a value that the new things cannot equal.

I love to go through the velvet box, finding pieces of all colors and of all sizes. And the ribbons of black velvet, some of them with white silk pecot edges, that were so popular long ago, used on every best dress. Everybody wore a black velvet bow somewhere, even tucked into a knot of hair on top of the head, or as a black velvet sash with long ends.

The trimming box fell apart long ago and now there are rolls of lace and cotton trimmings carefully laid away in my chest. Once a year, the stores used to have sales—real bargains—of trimmings, all-overs, and edgings, and that was the time the family stocked up. Waists and even hats were made of all-overs, the hats over wire frames. And every dress in those days was trimmed beyond possible comfort!

The odd snappers and hooks and eyes! My ancestors could never throw away any worn-out garment without first cutting off all the snappers or the hooks and eyes. And they match, too! Someone told of finding a box of snapper halves at an auction, which was probably saved for the day when the other half might turn up to make whole snappers! We have not had to buy snappers and hooks and eyes for fifty years or more. We keep them in boxes in our antique sewing table. All sizes in black and white are ready to be used when we sit down to sew or repair.

Old damask table cloths that long ago gave up their usefulness have once more come to light and sunshine. They can be dyed, cut into two pieces, and used as window draperies. Our luncheon cloths come from small pieces of damask table cloths and we make glass towels from parts. Even old homespun sheets with initials woven in one corner can be used as window draperies when dyed. A handwoven linen sheet was always made of two pieces sewed together in the middle. By ripping a sheet, you get two pieces which can serve as drapery for dining room, den, or bedroom; something money cannot buy. Green, yellow, or blue are attractive colors for both the damask table cloths and the homespun sheets.

You hear strange stories of new tenants finding piece boxes when they buy an old house, in attics and closets. There is a joy that younger generations can never know when there are piece boxes, drawers, and odds and ends and bits of this and that, which have been saved down the years. It is not a stingy trait, keeping things. To save is a thrifty trait that runs through many generations of the older families and their children and grandchildren.

47

THE OLD QUILTING PARTIES

And 'twas from Aunt Dinah's quilting party
I was seeing Nellie home.

WE HAVE BEEN SLEEPING UNDER QUILTS, PUFFS, AND ELECTRIC BLANKETS and we are grateful that we can keep warm. If our ancestors have left us one or two patchwork quilts, we have more reason to be grateful.

Patchwork was a thrifty way of using scraps of cloth. Without doubt, that was the reason we have had so much patchwork handed down to us. The women folk made that as their handwork, especially in the long winter months. The pieces were often cut by a pattern, either of tin or cardboard. Many quilts are artistic creations and many of the women were artists in color and design. They even gave the quilts names, from the designs.

The quilting bee was one of the social events of the winter. It took place in a large room, such as an attic room or a ballroom in one of those spacious homes. In the Sheldon Manse in Old Deerfield is a large room on the top floor, running the length of the house. Here the women gathered, not only for one afternoon but for many. It was a great event for them; a time when tongues flew as fast as the needle!

When the women arrived, they had with them a small basket in which was a small lace cap. They took off their big bonnets and shawls and put on the little lace cap, a custom which they always kept. In the front hall of the Andover Historical Society's beautiful eighteenth-century home, there hangs a small reed basket. This was what was used in bringing the lace cap to the quilting bee. One such basket is in my collection, minus its handle.

Arriving at the bee, the women set at once to their work; some to sew on patchwork and others to get ready for quilting. A lining of calico was laid on a table. Calico of long ago had beautiful and dainty patterns. On that went a thin layer of wool. And on that was laid the finished piece of patchwork. The edges were carefully basted. Then the quilting frame was set up. It was made of four narrow bars of wood, two sides and two ends alike, put together with four screw clamps, making a frame of the required size. This was laid on the backs of chairs. The quilt was carefully basted to the frame and the women began their quilting sitting around the frame.

Quilting party

Many times the sewing was done in fancy patterns as well as in straight lines, diagonal, or following the pattern of the patchwork in circles, flowers, or the like. Beautiful fine stitches went into the quilt, as we can see today.

After sewing a few hours, a repast was laid out on tables and it must have been a veritable feast: bread and butter, hot biscuits, sauce, preserves, doughnuts, all kinds of pie, and cheese and cakes. Tea was the drink. Then the groups left, to return the following day.

One quilt which is not often seen is the "friendship quilt." This was made of eight or ten squares of patchwork sewed together with a plain, white center. On each white square was the name, written in ink of the maker, a friend of the one for whom the quilt was made. Each of the 10 squares was sewed together, making a quilt of all those friends—a beautiful act of friendship. I saw such a friendship quilt on Martha's Vineyard, coming down from Duxbury, having the names of friends of Mother's classmate on each square. I have one on my bed with a center name of Mary Crocker.

Although we now resort to satin puffs and electrified blankets, many of us boast of one or more quilts, made a generation or two ago, when hand-work had not yet given over to machine work.

48

HOW OTHER GENERATIONS RESTED

AS FAR BACK AS HISTORY RECORDS, WE FIND THE WORD "BED," FOR MAN needed to rest at the end of the day.

The original use of the word applied to skins, rugs, straw, or rushes placed upon the floor. The word "bedstead" implied a frame on which were placed mattresses and coverings. The two words are now synonymous, meaning a place to sleep.

Turning back to the scribes at the time of the Bible, we find that the ancients used woven or plaited mats of straw or rushes, the latter known as bulrushes. In the book of Matthew, we read that Christ said, "Take up thy bed and go into thine house," which surely would have been this mat or rug. But again we read in Deuteronomy of the King Og of Bashan, a giant, who had a bedstead of iron. The frame was thirteen feet and eight inches long and six feet wide.

Another scribe, Luke, wrote that "no man when he lighted a candle . . . putteth it under a bed, but rather in a candlestick." This refers to a bedstead, a frame on legs.

Greek and Roman furnishings were pictured on painted vases and in sculpture unearthed from ruins of old cities. Those ancients had beds made in the form of a couch, partly of brass and partly of walnut wood. They were about 7½ feet long and 4 feet wide, standing 1½ feet high and having four or six legs.

A bed that became famous through Shakespeare's *Twelfth Night* is known as the Great Bed of Ware. This is now in Hertfordshire, England. It is 12 feet square and it held twelve people. It has an elaborately carved headboard and two elaborate posts at the foot of the bed. The roof of the frame is a solid board with heavily carved, narrow side pieces.

When the Pilgrim fathers built their homes in this country, there were two factors to contend with: lack of heat and lack of space. The tables were hutch tables or trestle tables. The hutch table top turned up and became the back of a settle or seat, having a compartment underneath, which was called a hutch and which gave the table its name. The top of a trestle table could be taken off and set up against the wall.

The turn-up bed came into existence as a space saver. The first and crudest form was a frame that fastened to the wall and hinged a distance of two feet from the head, allowing the bed proper to be swung up against the wall when not in use. This long part had two post legs at the end on which the frame rested when it was let down for use. The frame was strung with rope, laced through holes in the four rails. This was done with a rope or cord tightener and a long wooden peg. Such a bed is in the Old Iron Works house in Saugus, Massachusetts, and in many other such early houses.

Other types developed from this turn-up bed. One was a cupboard or press bedstead, so called because the bed shut up into a cupboard or press, entirely within the wall. Panelled doors shut over the bed or in some cases, the panelling was part of the floor of the bed. A few of these turn-up beds enclosed in a panelling are in existence today. One is in a home in the town of Petersham, north of Worcester. Another one came from the Sheldon homestead in Old Deerfield and is now in the museum of that town.

In Augusta, Maine, is another cupboard bed. Within the walls of the opening are compartments or secret places where papers and documents or money and valuables could be kept, unknown to outsiders. It is in the home of the grandfather of a friend of mine. She recalled sleeping in the bed one night, many years ago; and when she expressed the fear that the bed might shut up, the grandfather gave her a bell, telling her to ring it if she got caught! Modern apartments of small rooms have revived the cupboard or press bed and thereby economize on space.

A rare bedstead in the Old Iron Works House in Saugus, Massachusetts, is a turn-up bed which raises on hinges. The frame of the head section is fastened to the wall, about two feet wide, the width allowed for pillows. The body of the bed is hinged to the frame, and has two short post legs at the end on which the bed rested when opened.

The bed is about six feet wide, strung with rope. High above the head of the bed against the wall is a narrow canopy on a frame, extending about two feet and as long as the width of the bed. This is covered with heavy red tapestry. Tapestry drapery hangs down the sides to the floor, tied back like window draperies. One such bed is in the Metropolitan Museum in New York. When the bed is closed or turned up, it fits under the overhead canopy and the draperies at the side.

Following the bed of the Colonial days came a bed of the late 19th century, built like a cabinet. That was called a Murphy bed or a Cabinet

How other generations rested

bed. It was patented. It had a safety lock, iron legs that swung onto the floor, and a long plate glass mirror on the bottom of the bed that could be used when the bed was shut up in a perpendicular position. Clamps held the mattress and bed clothes when the bed was closed in the daytime.

History records that four-poster beds date back 2000 years. The American Colonies had such beds, beautifully carved, the earliest type having high posts, eight or nine feet high. An arched frame over the top connected the four posts. The covering over the frame was called a tester, made of net and bound with ball fringe or of chintz or copperplate cloth. Hanging from the rails of the bed to the floor was a valence, made of chintz or copperplate, matching the covering of the frame. The frame over the top was often flat instead of arched. Elaborate coverlets or matching chintz were used on the bed. Beautiful handwoven spreads were made and such heirlooms are highly prized today.

The more common four-poster beds have posts four or five feet high, made of maple, cherry, pine, or mahogany. The posts were turned on the lathe and some of them are beautifully cut, topped with a carved pineapple, an urn, or merely a ball. At the head of the bed is a solid board, while at the foot there is a board, or a rail, matching the posts. Skilled workmen made such beds, along with highboys, secretaries, tables, and chairs. The sleigh bed was still another type of bed with head and footboard fashioned like the dasher of a sleigh. These were made of mahogany.

An accompanying accessory to the big bed in the early kitchens was a trundle bed. This was a low bed with short posts and short legs. It slipped under the big bed in the daytime and was pulled out at night for the children to sleep in. Still another bed with short posts was one that could be placed under the eaves in the attic or in the lean-to. This was called the "hired man's" bed.

For a mattress, sacks of homespun linen were stuffed with straw, rushes, or corn stalks. Sometimes cattails were used as stuffing. These various stuffings were chopped and shredded, and when they became matted, new material was easily supplied. Feathers first came from wild turkeys, hawks, owls, or hens. The birds were killed and the soft feathers were taken for stuffing.

The more feather beds a housewife had, the better housewife she was considered. These were piled upon the bed, two or even three of them sometimes as a covering as well as a mattress. Bed steps were necessary to assist one to climb up into bed. Then the sheets were warmed with a warming pan and the occupant was fairly well protected during the cold night in an unheated room. Side curtains that hung down from the upper rail of the high four-poster beds could be drawn for further protection from the cold.

Homespun linen sheets came in due time and heavy hand-woven blankets were used. The sheets were made from home-grown flax and blankets were made from the wool of the sheep that each family raised. Quilts, coverlets, or counterpanes lined with wool gave ample protection from the cold. Feather pillows and bolsters added more comfort. Beautiful chintz or copperplate served as a spread over the bed, matching the ruffled valence that hung from the rails and the foot of the bed.

The evolution from the bed of skins to those of the modern day discloses a long process of many changes. Man made these for his comfort so that he might rest from his labors.

49

THE REAL COMFORT OF A FEATHER BED

UP IN OUR ATTIC IS A FEATHER BED. IT IS FULL SIZE, MADE FOR A FOUR-poster bed. It once belonged to my grandparents, and many times in the cold winters it has been dragged down and used on some of our beds; a few times on mine. You will never know what solid comfort you can have while sleeping until you have slept on a feather bed, all plumped up!

Back in the beginning of the Plymouth Colonies, the houses were cold, bleak, and bare. The only heat came from the cavernous fireplaces in the room, which at first was sitting room, work room and bedroom. There in that room was a bed, a turn-up bed that was fastened to the wall during the day, to be out of the way. The need of warm clothing was quite neces-sary and feather beds were made and used; not only one on a bed, but two and sometimes three, one often used as a covering for the sleeper.

The feathers for the bed were taken from wild birds and later from geese, when flocks were common to every household. The birds were plucked twice a year for the soft downy feathers that grew on the breast. Goose plucking must have been a terrible job. It is bad enough when housekeepers transfer feathers from one pillow to another, but to pluck a live goose, squirming and quacking, was something to be finished as soon as possible. A black cloth was tied over the head of the goose. The plucker held the bird high in the air by its feet, with one hand; the head of the goose was held between the knees, while with the other hand the feathers were plucked. Sometimes, the goose was held head down in a big splint basket called a goose basket; one such shaped like a big bottle with a cover, is in my collection.

Every day the feather bed had to be plumped up and shaken down again. Giving the bed a shaking in the morning was all in the day's work. Older generations tell of using a broom handle to smooth the feathers flat again. But there were wooden paddles made for that purpose, short

179

and thin with a handle. I had such a paddle in my collection for more than two years before I knew for what purpose it was used. It is a graceful thing, round at the end, showing wear at the sides. The initials T L are cut into one side. One day an elderly friend who had been brought up in the country visited me. In the course of our conversation, she said how a broom handle had been used in her day to smooth out the feather bed. My mind went quickly to the paddle I had. There, sure enough, was a feather bed smoother! It showed no signs of having been used as a scoop and the sides had been broken in some definite use. It took a deft flip of the wrist to use the paddle back and forth on the bed. The initials show that it was given to a young lady by her lover, as an engagement present or even as a wedding present. Presents in those days were practical in the extreme; often a splintered birch broom or a long-handled fry pan would be added as a good omen. I find I have three paddles now.

The real comforts of a feather bed

In the days of my grandparents, a feather bed was sometimes used under the hair mattress on top of the ropes of the bed frame. But more often it was on top of the mattress, covered with a quilt and a sheet over the quilt. Patchwork quilts and coverlids were piled one on the other to keep the occupant warm. The bedrooms had no heat and the nights were bitter cold. Feather pillows or bolsters were always used, too.

I can well imagine that up country on cold winter nights the extra feather beds are dragged down from the attic and put onto the beds.

They were often kept hanging on clotheslines to keep them out of reach of mice. Some families had splint baskets where they stored their beds in the summer. When the thermometer drops to zero and below, there is nothing more comfortable for a warm sleep than snuggling down into a feather bed.

50

THE PASSING OF THE CRADLE

MUCH HAS BEEN SAID ABOUT WALKING A CHILD TO QUIET IT AND COMFORT it. Once quieted, it is laid in its crib and it begins to cry again. It senses the change of position. Psychologists say that rocking the infant in a cradle is a logical way of putting it to sleep. Then there are no disturbing changes of position. Our ancestors must have known that, for every child was brought up in a cradle. From far back in history comes the expression "From the cradle to the grave."

The first cradle of the white man was made from a tree log. It could be rocked because of its round shape. The baby was tied in with a cord that ran through holes at the side and it could not roll out. Then cradles were made to swing on two posts, extending from standards like a hammock. The cradles were made of wooden slats or of reeds, like large and long baskets. In the era of black walnut, cradles were made to match the massive beds, with an oblong slatted frame and a solid headboard and footboard. These swung on standards and were very ornamental to any bedroom.

In the 17th and 18th centuries, it is said that master craftsmen designed the cradles as they did the furniture. These were often hooded and painted. The hoods were made with two slanting parts, giving the baby more headroom. The rockers were wide and short. If there happened to be twin babies, two hoods were made, one at each end, one for each baby.

The first time I saw a cradle with no footboard, I thought it had a missing part. Then I learned that some cradles were made with no footboard. In those early days, a child was dressed in swaddling clothes. Rather than fold or tuck in all the extra cloth, the long garments could extend out of the cradle when there was no footboard.

Cradles were rocked by the pressure of the mother's foot. She could sit in a chair, do her work, and keep the cradle in motion with her foot. If the child awakened, it was a simple matter to rock the cradle again.

The passing of the cradle

A large cradle, a grown-up size, has been seen—but rarely. This was made for some person who never matured mentally and who chose to sleep in the cradle as it did in its childhood.

An ingenious thing our ancestors did was to put rockers on a long settee. These are collector's items, with their Windsor spindles and decorated back bar. Then someone conceived the idea of having a place for the baby at one end of the long seat. A rack was made of spindles and painted to match the settee. This was set into holes at the edge of one end of the seat. It extended half the distance of the seat. In this protected space, the baby could be laid with a mattress, pillow, and blankets. Then the mother could sit at the other end with the baby lying by her and she could rock and do various pieces of work. If she were left-handed, the frame was set into holes at her left; if she were right-handed, it set into holes at her right.

Today, we see such racks or fences on beds for children as a protection from falling out. This is just one more example of how an idea born more than a century ago is taken over by today's manufacturers.

Cradles are found in poetry and song, but we saw the passing of them two generations and more ago.

51

HOW OUR ANCESTORS KEPT WARM

"AS THE DAYS BEGIN TO LENGTHEN, THE COLD BEGINS TO STRENGTHEN" is a saying oft repeated as soon as winter takes over. A report comes to us that the next 100 years will see milder weather and less precipitation, meaning less snow in winter. Meteorologists say that we have a cycle of seven years in our weather, each year building up to the seventh one, which is the most severe.

Centuries ago, when the first houses were built in the Northern climes in this country, it was a matter of much concern how to keep warm. The houses were built so that the door leading from the outdoors into the room with the big fireplace faced South. This was the direction from which came the most sunshine and the fewest cold blasts. Look at the old houses as you drive away from the city and notice how they face South. Quite often, an entry was added, giving extra protection. In an old unpainted clapboarded house in Still River, near the home of Bronson Alcott, there is a house with a square entry facing the road. This has two doors, one facing South and one facing West. The builder planned that on warm days, the West door could be used and on cold days, with snow and wind raging, the South door had less exposure. Such an arrangement is on the entry of the little old Quaker Church in Oxford, Massachusetts.

Those early houses were built with a peculiar insulation. Between the outside wall and the inside panelling a mixture of clay, chopped straw and crushed seashells was packed. This process was called nogging. More often than not, those first houses had no cellar. Any additional room was built with a cellar, but it was only for the purpose of storing. Between the first layer of boards on the ground and the inside floor boards, this mixture was packed for insulating. Insulation was thus conceived centuries ago. The few windows were small, placed high in the room. Plaster was made in later years, a combination of lime and sand mixed with hair, and this was put onto walls for further protection from the cold. Then much

later, in 1745, wallpaper appeared, both for decoration and for helping
to keep out the cold. When taking off wallpaper in an old room, one often
finds several layers, one put upon the other as the years went by. More
than that, ticking was often put onto the panelling before the wallpaper
was hung. A record discovery was ticking and thirteen layers of wallpaper.

Heat for the room was from logs, seven and eight feet long, burning
in the cavernous fireplace. Then Benjamin Franklin, a creative genius,
conceived the idea of stoves, with a pipe set into the chimney and the fireplace covered over with a sheet of cast iron. The Franklin stove and the
Franklin grate could burn wood or coal, giving out much heat. Following
these arrangements, many inventions of stoves came onto the market,
from those that were airtight to those that were large and pot-bellied,
placed in churches, stores, and other places where gatherings took place.

It is surprising how few of the modern generations have heard of
sandbags for windows, to keep out the cold. In my grandmother's time
and further back than that, the women made long, tubular bags, the length
across the window and an inch and a half wide. The strips of cloth were
sewed, turned right-side out on a yard stick, and then filled with sand.
The ends were tied. These were placed on window sills and at the top of
the lower sash by the lock, to keep out the cold air.

How our ancestors kept warm

We can prove that in our house, for I have made bags from old cloth in the piece box, filled them, and in cold winters I use them at three North windows and in the pantry window. A neighbor at one time used sand bags made of old red flannel and they lent a bit of color, seem from the streets. Perhaps all of this is old-fashioned, but many old ideas are worth much today.

There are still some families in the country, in exposed sections, who bank their cellars with leaves, all around the foundation, like their parents and grandparents did. That is old-fashioned, too, but it keeps a lot of cold from going into the cellar.

Today, we are keeping warm in our over-heated homes and we are using little effort to keep comfortable, twenty-four hours a day. We do not have to think up ingenious devices—they are handed out to us and installed for use. But are we the hardy race our ancestors were or are we avoiding any effort and being pampered too much?

52

THE COMING OF CLOSETS

STEP INTO AN OLD HOUSE THAT HAS BEEN REMODELED AND YOU WILL find nary a closet. A large pantry with a window, a butt'ry, or a milk room equally as large, but as for small closets, there are none.

Chests, settles, hutch tables, and highboys came into being because of the dire need for storing. Our generation is blessed with this heritage and we pride ourselves on having them, never once thinking of how they were needed in the long-ago days of our ancestors.

The first holder for household linens and the many coverlids and blankets was a chest. It stood on the floor with no legs. It was beautifully made and decorated—with carved scrolls, a date, and the initials of the one for whom it was made.

When a young woman married two and three generations ago, she came to her new home with a large dowry. Not to show wealth, but for the need of much household linen did she spin, weave, and make countless sheets, pillow cases, and other linens and wool blankets. She knew there could be little laundering and the linen would have to carry over from month to month. A place to store this dowry was important and it was the chest that was the first storage place.

Many chests were made by master craftsmen; one particular joiner lived in old Hadley, Massachusetts. His chests were called Hadley Chests. Sailors on the high seas had a chest of their own, with lock and key and an inner compartment, for private papers. Often the chest was made in a foreign land from native woods, especially from camphor wood, found in China, Japan, and the Indies and brought back to this country. One such large chest is in our family; it is beautifully made, with brass corners, heavy brass handles, a brass nameplate, and a brass lock and key. We also have a sailor's chest, painted gray with rope handle. Both of these chests stand on the floor.

The high-back settle that stood by the fireplace had a boxed-in compartment under the seat. The hutch table had a similar compartment. "Hutch" means a bin or holder and when the table top was lifted, a settle was made; when closed, a table. Both of these compartments were for storing. There were chests on chests, but the highboy stood high on slender legs, with an upper set of drawers and small drawers in the lower part. Made by master craftsmen, highboys were extremely beautiful. A fan decorated the lower single drawer and often the center of the top drawer. The two curved sides of the top rolled over to the center to make what was called a bonnet top. In the center of the roll, a pineapple or an urn ornament was placed. Sometimes, an open-work railing went around the top of the highboy, if it were flat. Highboys were made of various woods—mahogany, maple, cherry, or pine. All of this furniture came because of the need for storing.

The coming of closets

It was perhaps because the housewife found it was not easy to clean under and around these early chests that bracket feet and legs to raise the chests from the floor appeared.

The change in the style of houses brought closets by the nineteenth century. Go into a house built 100 years ago or earlier and you will find closets galore. Chimney closets, china closets, under-the-stairs closets, and kitchen closets. Even then the hat-tree stood or hung in the front hall and a costumer was commonly found in a bedroom.

About 100 years ago, the wardrobe appeared. Our family had one that was made of two sides and a top, built into a corner of a bedroom. It had a door and upper and lower hooks. Up in our attic—I love to think of the interesting things up there—is a real wardrobe. The base has two long drawers, with wooden knobs, and the top rests on this base. In the top are two doors opening upon an array of hooks. The wardrobe stands about eight feet high, with a most attractive flaring top, made of pumpkin pine, grained the color of mahogany.

Then came the smaller houses, small apartments, and consequentially small closets. If women could be the designers, perhaps there would be plenty of closet room. But lack of space and an eye for beauty makes for small closets or few closets. Chests are called upon once more to help out.

53

TRUNKS FROM A TREETRUNK

IN OUR ATTIC STOREROOM, THERE ARE SOME TRUNKS OF VARIOUS SORTS and various ages. One of them has been kept over the years because it was the trunk father had in the Civil War, Father enlisted in the band when he was 17 years old, playing the cornet. His trunk is about 18 inches long, 8 inches wide and 7 inches deep. It is covered with leather, fastened with brass studs, and it is lined with wallpaper. It has a lock and key. It is not unlike many of the trunks made in that period from 1800 to 1875. Several such trunks are in our family, one measuring only a foot long, all covered with leather, and having a lock and key, often a padlock.

The word "trunk" comes about naturally. A piece of a trunk of a tree was taken—a tree about 16 or 18 inches in diameter—the log air-dried and stripped of its bark. One side was flattened for the bottom. A slice on the opposite side was taken off for a cover. The inside of both bottom and cover was scooped out with a cutting tool to a thinness. The cover was then set back onto the bottom with two wire hinges; those first hinges were shaped at home. The lock was a hasp, with a key or padlock. That was man's first trunk. Many were covered with animal skin, first from the wild deer and later from domestic animals like the calf.

Traveling was seldom attempted in those early days because the connection between one town and another was little more than a path. Peddlers were the first to seek communication, first on foot and then on horseback. They carried tin trunks filled with their wares, measuring fully twenty-three inches long and fifteen inches wide and as much deep. These were slung over their shoulders by means of straps of webbing, homespun. Riding on horseback, the peddlers carried one or two trunks across the backs of the horses. The word *peddler* was often spelled *pedlar*.

In due time, trunks were made from slabs of wood, still with a round top and covered with animal's skin, either deer or calf. The hair is still seen on the old covered trunks, showing from which animal the skin was

Trunks

taken. The skin was fastened on with small brass tacks and often the tacks were used in putting on the initials and the date.

Stagecoach traveling brought about a demand for trunks and they became more numerous. Along with the trunks went band boxes, another part of the old days. Stagecoach passengers could carry a limited amount of baggage—twenty-three pounds to a person. The era of the stagecoach was a colorful one, what with all the hazards of traveling in any and all weather, and carrying mail as well as passengers.

From trunks made from a log and then tin and then slabs, progress went on to those of the Gay Nineties; with a flat top, bound with metal, and held together by straps, clamps, and a lock.

Sailors on the high seas had chests. Often, the men made them after they had landed on a foreign shore, using native woods. Chests made of camphor wood are highly prized today. Such wood was found in the East Indies and in Japan. Made of wide boards and a boxed cover, they were often made stronger with brass corners, with a brass nameplate on the cover. They were made in as many sizes as was deemed necessary. One in my bedroom is a large one, with brass corners, heavy brass handles, and a brass nameplate, smelling strongly of camphor. I used to think Mother had put mothballs into it, until I became versed in antiques!

Inside the chests there was always a compartment with a cover built into one end. This was used to hold special papers or documents but never had a lock and key.

Ordinary chests for sailors were plain boxed affairs, commonly painted gray. They had a lock and key and for handles there were cleats of wood at each end through which a piece of rope was strung. That was the typical handle of the sailor's chest.

Baggage has taken a tremendous stride—from the first trunk made from a log of a tree to the great variety carried in automobiles today. Traveling brings the necessary equipment.

PART IV
WHEN WE WERE VERY YOUNG

54

THE DAYS OF LIMITED SCHOOLING

WITH THE CONSTANT DISCUSSION OF EDUCATION AND SCHOOLS AND colleges, with the changes that are taking place in curriculums and standards, we realize the vast strides education has made since early Colonial days.

It hardly seems possible that girls were not allowed to enter the town's district school until the year 1788. The privilege of a public education was not granted to them until long after the Reverend John Harvard made possible the establishing of Harvard College for boys. It sounds strange to read, "Who will cook our food and mend our clothes if girls are to be taught philosophy and astronomy?" Or again, "If you expect to become widows and carry pork to market, it may be well enough to study mental arithmetic. Otherwise, keep to the womanly branches." A few private schools were in existence where girls were taught all the stitches in sewing, how to read and how to recite the many catechisms, but they were limited in number.

The Governor of Hartford was quite distressed because his wife, in 1645, had "fallen into a sad infirmity . . . by giving herself wholly to reading and writing . . . If she had attended her household affairs and such things as belong to women, and not gone out of her way and calling to meddle in such things as belong to men whose minds are stronger, she had kept her wits and might have improved them usefully and honorably in the place God had set her."

There were no slates or copy books for at least 100 years after the first schools had been established. The alphabet was taught by rhymes. Here is one given to a class in arithmetic:

> A gentleman a chaise did buy,
> A horse and harness, too;
> They cost the sum of three score pounds,
> Upon my word, 'tis true.

The harness came to half the horse,
The horse twice the chaise,
And if you find the price of them,
Take them and go your ways.

In one school down Maine, so my "adopted grandmother" told me, the multiplication table was sung to the tune of Yankee Doodle. (Try it and see how it goes.)

Five times five are twenty-five,
Five times six are thirty,
Five times seven are thirty-five
And five times eight are forty.

In the one-room school house, heat in the winter came from a large fireplace. Eventually, this was replaced by a stove that stood in the middle of the room. A wood box out in the entry supplied the fuel, but more often than not the wood was green and the fire seldom burned without much tending. When only boys were allowed to go to school, each boy had to furnish half a cord of wood. If he failed to do so, he could not sit near the stove to keep warm.

The teacher had a high desk and a high stool and the pupils sat on wooden benches; the girls on one side and the boys on the other. The teacher's life was not a happy one, for he not only had little pay, but boarded from one house to another, taking whatever fare was given to

The days of limited schooling

him, free. Those first teachers were young men with little education. The teacher had to do odd jobs to eke out his living. He was the head of the singing school, he led the church choir, he helped the farmers in any and all work and he was even a grave digger.

The school term varied in different sections. Some towns had summer sessions, with no school during the winter months on account of the severe weather. Other schools began in the fall, closed during the winter months, and began in the spring. This was all because of the severe winters with deep snows. School kept six days, beginning early in the morning and closing at 5 in the afternoon, or 4 in the winter months. The noontime recess was two hours in length and the pupils, who did not have to spend the time in reviewing work, went out to slide and skate on the nearby ponds. For sliding, a wooden bench was turned over and that made a fine toboggan. The girls seldom had skates, but the boys pulled them around as they slid on their feet. A collection of those skates, with wooden bottoms and metal runners ending in a curve far out front, are examples of the handwork of the village blacksmith.

The noon time lunch box played an important part in the day at school. Cakes, cookies, doughnuts, pies, and home-made bread and butter made up the assortment, with little thought of the necessity for the proper food for growing children. We do not hear of milk in the tin lunchbox, so we assume that the drink came from the tin dipper out in the entry and the old wooden pump out in the yard.

As time went on, school closed Saturday noon, giving the children an extra half day. Then came the full Saturday of freedom, time given to helping on the farm. No mention is made of any vacation at the time of the Christmas Holidays, except the one day. In spite of the severe discipline in those old schools, many fine men and women emerged and became pioneers in their fields. They produced equally fine offspring, too.

Somewhere, a generation or two ago, a rhyme sprung up and it has echoed down the years. When the last day of school came, we used to sing out:

No more Latin, no more French,
No more sitting on the hard wood bench.
No more learning, no more books,
No more teacher's cross-eyed looks!

What a contrast the schooling of today is to that of yesterday! Women as well as men have explored every known field and have gone their way unhampered.

55

OLD SCHOOL SLATES

THERE'S A LITTLE RED SCHOOL HOUSE DOWN IN SOUTH SUDBURY, MASSA-chusetts. It has only one room and it is red because the paint made from the clay in the soil was all that was known in the old days.

That one-room school house was moved from Sterling to South Sudbury (by the late Henry Ford) onto the property of the Wayside Inn. He wanted to preserve it for future generations. It was in that little red school house that there was a Mary who had a little lamb that followed her to school one day. Sarah Josepha Hale, editor of *Godey's Lady's Book,* wrote a poem about the devoted lamb that made the school hallowed.

For many years, that little red school house was used on its new location. The old wooden pump stands at one side. A stone with a brass plaque tells the history of the schoolhouse. There were sixteen children of the first four grades and a teacher for several years. Now, it stands in silence; its duties have passed into history.

Do you ever come across an old school slate, bound with a red cord? Whenever one does turn up it is coveted by someone who delights in the memories that school slates bring back. The red binding was put on to deaden the noise of the slates as they were moved around on the desks. The school room was not the quietest place in the village, with the children of various ages learning their readin', 'ritin', and 'rithmatic. The red cord on those old slates was laced through holes around the wooden frame of the slate. At a later time, the red cord was nailed to the edge of the frame, showing another period of time. Occasionally, you might find two slates bound with red cord hinged together. That made four surfaces on which to write.

Many slates were made in the days of the old school houses. Slate was taken from quarries and sold commercially to manufacturers who cut the pieces into various sizes, polished them with pumice, and framed them in wood. Some frames were made with rounded corners, others with squared corners, mitred together. Nearly always, an old slate has some mark of ownership on it. Initials or names were cut into the wood with a jackknife or inked on it. Some slates have a strap of leather or a colored cord strung through a hole in the middle of one end, so the slate could be hung.

When once you begin to collect slates, you are surprised at the many kinds. One in my family can be traced back 100 years. It is a thin sheet of parian marble, framed in a black leather binding. On one edge is a slot which holds the pencil; a lead pencil, for marble would not take a pencil made of slate.

Production of slates began as early as 1812. The output of both slates and slate pencils reached a peak in the middle of the 19th century, the slates totalling about 600 a day. The first pencils were made by pressing the moistened slate powder until it was firm enough to be made into sticks, slender and four or five inches long. A few years later, pencils in wooden cases appeared. A half cylinder of wood with a groove in it was packed with slate powder. Then the other half was glued onto that. Such pencils lasted much longer and were not easily broken.

Old school slates

A rare desk slate was discovered in an antique shop. Closed, it looks like a writing desk of black walnut that was so popular 50 to 75 years ago, with a slanting top which opened. The slate desk has a slanting top of a framed slate, ten inches long and eight inches wide. The lid is opened by pressing a pin which releases a catch. Inside are three compartments: two are for pencil, compass, ruler, and sponge eraser; the other is for copy sheets of thin pieces of wood, eight by two inches wide, painted black and numbered. Each sheet has a separate set of designs to copy, such as houses, faces, and household articles such as tubs, pitchers, crockery dishes, and urns. Other sheets have words and sentences. All of these designs are sketched in white. The name C. C. Shepard is on a label on the bottom, dated 1877.

Another single slate has its copy sheets of cardboard set into a frame that is attached to the edge of the slate. On these are many pictures. The frame can be raised when the copying is being done and closed when put away. On the back of the frame is a slot with a ruler. Still another slate has copy material on the four sides of the wide, wooden frame. Since there was printing on both sides of the slate, this made for eight sets of copy.

In my family there was once a slate book. It went the way of many things that were called old and worn out. It measured about eight inches long and four inches wide, with three leaves. The leaves are bound into the book with cloth strips. These were made of a composition; doubtless silica or quartz pressed into sheets. The name of New York Silicate Book Slate Co. is printed on the cover of a similar slate book in my collection.

About that time, there were slates made with a piece of frosted glass set into a frame. Any picture could be put under the glass to copy, with a lead pencil. There was a scroll slate, too, that had frosted glass over a paper scroll. The rolls were turned by knobs, which brought different pictures to copy in view. The pictures are barnyard animals. This again was put out by Shepard and patented in 1874.

An unusual slate is in the collection of Nina Fletcher Little of Essex, Massachusetts. It is made of three separate slates, hinged to each other, about a foot long and eight inches wide. Two of the slates have a wooden back, so when closed over the middle slate, the whole gives the appearance of a box. On the edge of one of the covers is a pouch for a slate pencil. To all appearances, it was used in a Village store.

Anyone owning a collection of slates can visualize the little red school house and the old wooden pump out in the yard. Within the room were the benches and later the desks and chairs, the old wood stove in one corner, the big brass bell on teacher's desk, and the tin dipper hanging out in the entry. Or you can think of yourself as a child, bending over your slate, laboriously making copies of the various drawings or creating your own.

In those long ago days of school, every child struggled with the daily readin', 'ritin', and 'rithmatic.

56

WHEN ROOFS WERE COVERED WITH SLATE

ALL TOO SELDOM DOES A PERSON DOING RESEARCH HAVE AN OPPORTUNITY to sit with one of the older generation and learn first hand of the old days. This has happened to me more than once and the story which follows is another bit of history that actually took place.

The narrator told me of his grandfather who owned a farm of many acres in Worcester. One spring, in the year of 1885, he wanted more cows for his herd. He set out in horse and buggy to drive to northern Vermont, taking a helper with him. Having purchased his cows, some twenty or thirty of them, he began his trip back home. The grandfather and the helper, called a cattle drover, took turns riding and walking with the cattle on their return. Stopping along the way at the end of each day, they put the cows out to pasture and rested in some farm house. Making a stop in Rutland, Vermont, they were surprised to have the farmer host ask if he might buy two or three cows from the lot. The farmer said he had no money but could give him something the next time. The deal was made and the cows were left behind. On a second trip, the farmer told the grandfather he still had no money. But out in his back yard, he went on to say, was a vein of rock which had been judged to be slate. The farmer agreed to have some men quarry it and he would pay his debt by giving him all the slate that could be taken. Four of five wagon loads went back home for the grandfather, in exchange for the cows.

The barn down in Worcester needed a new roof and the grandfather went to work to cut the slates and put them on. After he had finished the job, a neighbor saw how well the roof looked and he asked if there were more slates so that he might have his barn slated. That was the beginning of one of the oldest roofing companies in Worcester. Many such chance happenings have been the means of the beginning of a new business.

To go on with my story, I found out that when my father built our house in 1878, the slates came from that Company. They are still intact

201

with but little repair done over the years. That roofing company has kept all of its old records and when looking over some early ones, the grandson found a paid bill for a repair of our roof. One slate was put on, valued at nine cents. Nails and so forth were extra. But a surprising statement came at the end. "No charge was made for cartage, for we walked to the job!"

It is up in Vermont that the oldest slate quarries are found. From Rutland over to Troy, New York, is a long range of hills which contain veins of slate. The layers run at an angle of about 80 degrees slant. The sheets were split by hand by skilled workers called quarriers. Quite often such work ran in one family for several generations.

When roofs were covered with slate

The first slates for roofs were large, as long as 24 inches and as wide as 14 inches. They were cut thin, but naturally of different thinness. When laid on a roof they overlap. The second row overlaps about half way over the first, and the third row, besides lapping over the second, laps about an inch or two over the first. This prevented any rain from penetrating between the cracks. Slates were laid over boarding, with a layer of tar paper first and then nailed with galvanized nails that did not rust.

From Bangor, Pennsylvania, came slate for school slates. These were quarried as early as the beginning of the 19th century. In these veins, lime was found to be a large percentage of the content. Bands or streaks of lime show white in the slate. This impurity did no harm in school slates. But if such slates containing lime were used outdoors, exposed to the air and elements, the lime would begin to crumble inside of 15 or 20 years. One such slate was brought into the office for me to see how a vein of lime in an otherwise perfectly good slate crumbled by merely touching it. Thus, those veins in Pennsylvania could be used only for school slates. Red or a brownish color slate was also found in Vermont. Such slates were used to make a fancy roof. In my collection of eighteen slates, there is one of reddish brown.

Thus my slate roof and my collection of school slates seemed to be of greater value after I had sat with that business friend who told me the story of slate.

57

PENNY CANDY AND SPENDING MONEY

THERE USED TO BE A CORNER STORE NEAR US UP ON MAIN STREET WHERE we children went to spend our penny. The owner was not too friendly nor was he particularly interested in us. I never remember that he talked to us. But we were so eager to pick out our penny's worth of candy that we did not notice that anything was lacking in the manner of our reception.

Our eyes came on level with the showcase. And did they open wide as we pointed out this and this and this while we were deciding what to buy! Small candy bananas of the most vivid hue, small chocolate pipes, sugar cigarettes with a bright bit of tinsel to represent a flame, white seed-covered flat chocolates, long licorice whips, licorice pipes, and a variety of other kinds.

We could read the mottoes on the pink and white heart-shaped candies; "He Loves Me," "Be My Valentine," "Are You My Sweetheart?" Sugared slices of orange and lemon gum candies, striped peppermint sticks, plain chocolate creams, little tin dishes with candy to be eaten with a tiny tin spoon, and lemon drops were all there. It took us a long time to decide what we would buy with our penny or perhaps two pennies. Some of the candy was a cent apiece, some were two for a cent and I can remember when we chipped in our pennies and could get six for five cents. One thing I recall about the conical chocolate creams: We would take off the round bottom and eat out the cream inside with a toothpick! Probably to make it last longer.

And well do I remember the round jar of pickled limes and the big barrel of pickles that stood on the floor by the counter! Why we children would choose a pickled lime or a huge juicy pickle, I could not say now, but how I did love the pickled lime then!

A penny or two a week was our allotment. We were never refused when we asked for a penny to spend, but quite often we earned our pennies. I remember pulling dandelions and plantain leaves from the lawns and I had a penny for a dozen roots. If we went on errands, we were given a penny. We learned to save them, putting them in our iron bank; a little green house guarded by a man we called Peter. He swung around after we had put the penny on his plate and he dropped it into the slot. Collectors are looking for such money banks!

Another time we bought candy was on Memorial Day. We walked to the cemetery and we passed a stand on a piazza, loaded down with candy for sale. The railing was like a trellis and we climbed up to see the display. (I still pass that piazza today!) Daddy was with us and he was generous; we took plenty of time to pick out a whole bag full. It was a striped bag.

Today's Country Stores are making a big hit with the counter of penny candy. Of course the supply has increased since the Gay Nineties, but the assortment is all there. What a thrill the oldsters have as they gaze at the candy and pick and choose; grandmas, grandpas, and parents. They may be buying for the children with them or for the children at home. They might even admit that they were taking a striped bag full just in fond remembrance of their lost childhood.

Penny candy and spending money

Where are today's pennies? The scale of compensation has risen along with all commodities. A nickel, a quarter, fifty cents, or even a dollar goes for spending money. No favors are given today without good pay; running an errand brings at least a nickel. The other day, our lawn was covered with small twigs blown from the elms in a high wind. Two neighbor children were helping pick them up while the grass was being cut. "Gimme a nickel if I pick up the sticks?" I agreed, but when the work was half done, the children quit and I had to finish.

What an assortment of packaged snacks goes over the counter today!

Any time you walk down the street you see babies, children, and teen-agers eating from a small cellophane package. Potato chips can be bought in small sizes, molasses-coated corn, cheese-coated corn, cheese bits of various shapes, and other varieties that appear on the counter overnight. All for ten or twenty-five cents! And ice cream goes over the counter to-day at a terrific rate, along with the various concoctions made from coated ice cream.

The penny did not stretch; it disappeared. The demands for spending did stretch and it is here to stay.

58

WITH MARBLES AND JUMP ROPES WINTER IS GONE

BEFORE THE LAST PILE OF SNOW HAS DISAPPEARED AND THE LAST MUD hole has dried up, you know spring has come by the gathering of the neighborhood boys hovering over a game of marbles. And when girls begin to swing jump ropes, winter is over.

Marbles date back to the Roman children who used nuts. The old word for the game was "mibs" and it is mentioned in the writings of Ovid. The rules were the same as those followed today but the names of the marbles have changed. The most valuable marbles were made of alabaster, called "allets." Stone marbles were called "stoneys" and those of clay were called "common eye." Today's names include some of the old, with some of the new added. Such famous factories as the Sandwich works made glass marbles when they were turning out paper-weights and door knobs. They made marbles of large sizes and collectors of things long since disappeared are accumulating beautiful specimens of glass marbles.

One of the sports not played today is hoop rolling. It was commonly seen until about 50 years ago, but now only an occasional Senior class in college performs on a special day. Hoop rolling was an English sport and grown-ups as well as youths had their hoops and sticks. The hoops were made of ash with the bark left on, until in later years, the manufacturers produced a smooth splinterless hoop. A person became quite skillful with hoop rolling, a favorite stunt being to dash in and out through the hoop while it was rolling at full speed. Competition waxed high when school clashes came in the spring; both sides tried to knock down the hoops of the opponents.

Tops are seen but seldom today. Top-spinning was an ancient game in the days of the Romans and in the Far East. A century ago, there were three types of tops; a top that had a cord that was wound around it, the top that was wound with a mechanical tip and then freed, and the musical top. The musical top was made of tin, gaily decorated in color, larger than the wooden tops. With it came a tin tray on which it was spun. Striking the top button while the top was in motion made a different note; the trick was not to knock over the top while changing the music.

Hop-scotch used to be called Scotch-hoppers. There has been little change in the pattern marked out in the dirt. There are ten spaces with an arrangement of combined skipping and resting. The last space, the dome, has had various names such as "cat's face," "the pudding" and "the Temple." And there the player rests.

Where is the man who never played pick knife or stick knife as a young boy? It used to be called mumblety-peg because the winner could drive a peg into the ground with three blows of the knife handle and the loser had to pull it out with his teeth. The knife rested in a dozen different ways as it was tossed into the ground and it had to land at a position so that at least two fingers could be put under it. Girls also joined in this sport.

With marbles and jump ropes, winter is gone

But the girls' favorite game was jack stones. This game was known in Greece 2000 years ago, as shown by paintings, and the stones were bones as well as pebbles. Other names for the game were chuck-stones and five-stones, because originally there were five stones used. All sorts of stunts were done with the fingers and hands to make a difficult game. A rubber ball came into the game in later years and the number of stones increased to ten.

Games and sports not listed as being common were often found locally. Remember the trick of swinging a pail full of water? You tied a stout cord to the handle of an empty lard pail and the trick lay in the beginning of the swing and at the stopping point, in not spilling the water and getting a ducking.

A lard pail cover served as a hoop to roll. A hole was punched through the middle of the cover, a bent nail was inserted, and a string was tied to the head of the nail. Starting the cover with a push, you ran as fast as you could, keeping the string taut and the cover on a slant.

Those old childhood games and stunts! They taught us to be skillful and quick. The joy of achievement was indelibly imprinted on our minds. There is a revival of many of the sports today, for some of them can never entirely pass out.

PART V
OLD TIME CUSTOMS AND FOLKLORE

59

BETWEEN YOU'N ME AND THE GATEPOST

ISN'T IT FUNNY HOW WE USE VARIOUS EXPRESSIONS AND HAVE NO IDEA where they came from! So many old sayings pop into our conversation and when we stop to think what they mean, we can only say, "Why, I've always heard that as far back as I can remember!"

It is quite common to say you did something "on your own hook," meaning that you did it by yourself and got away with it. The real meaning dates back to the days of the early settlers. They went out in fishing boats to catch cod, to provide both food and the oil for light. Young boys who began as apprentices were allowed all the fish they caught on their own hook.

When we say "by hook or by crook" we are predicting that we will get whatever we want by hooking it, regardless of whether it is the proper thing for us to have and regardless of the methods we employ.

To "go the whole hog" means we go the limit, the entire amount. Our ancestors scalded a whole hog after killing it, roasted a whole hog on the spit in the fireplace, and served a whole hog, stuffed, with an apple in its mouth. There were large wooden platters on which whole hogs were served—the one in my museum measures a yard long, with a rim five inches deep. A whole hog was served roasted, stuffed, with feet and tail and head left on, an apple in its mouth for decoration.

A "Sabbath Day's journey" was actually about a mile in distance. Common usage makes it an all-day's journey. And "once in a blue moon" comes from the Chinese. A blue moon has never happened so that "once" means it will never happen.

We are left "high and dry" when misfortune comes and the tide goes out and there is nothing to hold onto. Perhaps luck returns with the tide or perhaps not. Or we "jump out of the frying pan into the fire," one place as bad as the other. And we surely have found ourselves "between the Devil and the deep sea," wondering which way was best to take.

The Devil has been given various names, such as "the Old Scratch," the "Old Harry," and the "Old Nick," used in the sense of behavior. "Little Johnny acts like the Old Harry!"

" 'Twixt you, me, and the gate-post."

When a horse was fed with his oats, he felt pretty good. Hence comes the saying that a person "feels his oats." When the Colonists first began to paint their houses—with paint they had to make themselves from the clay in the soil—the neighbors used to say, "John's painted his house. He feels his oats!" That was not complimentary!

You have heard of crocodile tears when a person pretends sorrow. A crocodile weeps when he eats his victim and it is far from an expression of sorrow.

How many names we have for a person we dislike! They are "crazy as a loon." Have you ever seen a loon's antics or heard its hideous laugh at night? A person is often a "stick-in-the-mud" when he is lazy and slow. Or maybe we say he is "as blind as a bat" when he fails to see something very obvious. Bats are blind in daylight. A person is "sweet as honey" or "quick as a cat" or as "slow as cold molasses." Perhaps we know a "namby pamby," a person who is weak and childish.

How many of us give a "lick and a promise" to a job when we cannot take the time for a thorough piece of work! Perhaps that sprang from the idea of a housekeeper of years ago who did not relish spending time on housecleaning in the proper way!

Originally "up the spout" meant that something had been put into pawn. Another way of saying that was "gone where the woodbine twineth" or gone "at my uncle's." Today a thing has "gone up the spout" when it has been lost, worn out, or thrown away.

It is "pitch dark" or "black as pitch" when the lights go out. The old use of the word pitch meant "to darken." Hence our interpretation of it. "Dark as a pocket" does not need any explanation.

How often we hear of someone being "sold down the river!" That originally was "gone up Salt River," an actual river in England. This meant a political defeat when the party was vanished. Now this is said more in the form of any dirty trick that has hurt someone.

"Fresh as a daisy," "Pretty as a pink," "Sweet as honey," "Pale as a ghost," "Thin as a rail," "Hard as nails," "Straight as a ramrod." It would be interesting to see how many different sayings come to mind as we recall these few!

60

MOTHER'S SUNDAY AS IT USED TO BE

EVERY YEAR, ON THE SECOND SUNDAY IN MAY, WE ARE MAKING NOTE of Mother's Sunday. This is a special Sunday which was set aside in Philadelphia on May, 10, 1908, at the request of a woman, Miss Anna Jarvis, after the loss of her mother. Five years later, Pennsylvania decreed that the second Sunday in May be set aside as a State observance. In 1913, Congress proclaimed it to be a National observation. It is an important day in the home, when we pay tribute to our living mothers and honor those gone from the home circle; a colored carnation for those living and a white carnation for those gone.

Three centuries ago, in rural England, there was a Sunday called Mothering Sunday. It was in 1643 that a Sunday in Lent was set aside when young people were admonished to carry wafers to their mothers and to visit them. The day was called Midlent Sunday and Wafering Sunday. The custom of setting aside such a Sunday was carried on for several generations, being recorded as late as 1791 when children as well as young people were offering wafers to their mothers.

A wafer was a form of unleavened bread used in ceremonies. As early as 1358, a wafer iron used in making wafers was mentioned in an appraisal of goods belonging to an English gentleman: "One pair of irons for the Eucharist." The wafers were taken with wine at the sacrament of the Lord's Supper.

A wafer iron or tongs is an iron utensil with two hinged parts, hand-wrought by the blacksmith. It has two round heads or plates, measuring about six inches in diameter, with handles three feet or more long. All implements used over the fire had long handles to allow the worker to stay back from the heat. Some early irons bear a seal with three locked hearts surmounted by a cross enclosed in a circle, and an anchor with ornaments imitating leaves. Other irons have a crucifix or a sacred monogram. The patterns are incised and the figures are made in the reverse

216

on the cakes. One such wafer iron in my museum is dated 1785, having initials W C M, a heart and a scroll on one head, while on the other are two hex marks and a simple scroll. The initials would appear to be the giver, the groom, for a wafer iron was included in the gifts to a bride. It was an omen of good luck.

The wafers or wafer cakes were made by a waferer and two or three irons were sufficient in supplying a community for any ceremony. It must have been a tedious task for one man to manage the irons and make a large number of cakes. The iron was first heated over a charcoal fire or in the embers of a fireplace, before the batter was put into the heads. Rests have been found on which long-handled implements could be placed while cooking over the fire. These rests are frames with three or four legs from which extend an arm to hold the handle of the cooking implements. The irons were extremely heavy and these rests relieved the worker from holding them.

As the years went on, the types of wafer irons changed and various shaped heads appeared. Some were oval; others were round. A short-handled wafer iron shows that wafers continued to be made when stoves replaced fireplaces.

In this country, the wafers were used in the home as well as in the church. The irons were made by local blacksmiths, with patterns on the heads, of flowers, initials, and dates, and the all-necessary hex mark. That mark was supposed to keep away the evil spirits, and witches in particular, and was used on doors, tools, and utensils to protect the owner. Among the Dutch, the mark is in the form of a circle around five petals, done with a compass.

A rule for making wafers or wafer cakes is given in a cook book

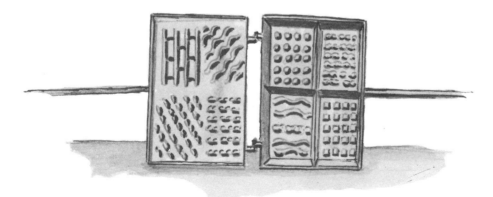

Mother's Sunday as it used to be

called *Two Fifteenth-Century Cookery Books.* "Waffres—Take the womb (belly) of a luce (full-grown pike) and sethe here wyl and do it on a mortar and tender cheese thereto, grynde them togethir; then take flour and whites of Eyren (obsolete word for eggs) and beat togethir and look that the eyroun (iron) be hot and lay thereon a thin paste and then make waffrys and so on." The bracketed explanations are mine.

From a cookbook of the early 19th century, it would seem that wafers continued to be used. By then, they were eaten in the home as well as in church ceremonies. A rule reads: "Dry the flour well which you intend to use, mix a little pounded sugar and finely pounded mace with it; then make it into a thick batter with cream; butter the wafer irons, let them be hot; put a teaspoonful of batter into them, so bake them carefully and roll them off the iron with a stick." Sometimes the rolled wafers were filled with whipped cream and sealed at the ends with a preserved strawberry.

Waffles and waffle irons are more commonly known than wafers and wafer irons; perhaps because they are used today. The two heads on long handles were at first oblong in shape, later changing to hearts and fancy patterns in the heads. In the early centuries, there was a Waffling Sunday in Sweden similar to the Wafering Sunday in old England. On that particular Sunday, the people of the various communities went from one home to another where they were served waffles. It was a social gathering of the communities.

A rule for waffles used more than one hundred years ago reads: "One quart flour and a teaspoon salt. One quart sour milk with two teaspoonsful of melted butter in it. Five well-beated eggs. A teaspoon or more of salaratus, enough to sweeten the milk. Bake in a waffle iron. Waffle irons well oiled with lard each time they are used."

Such records of the early years bring to us of the 20th century a history of that first Mother's Sunday. Three hundred years ago, the observance was established. Love, honor, and respect brought about the day and in this modern world, there should be that same love, honor, and respect.

61

THE MOON IN ALL ITS GLORY

WHEN WE WERE YOUNG WE USED TO SING OUT AT THE TIME OF THE FULL moon:

> Moony, moony, shine on me,
> Make me spoony as I can be!

What romance there is in the full moon! Moonlight changes the aspect of everything about us and makes objects and shadows seem unreal. The sharp shadows make fantastic shapes. Little wonder that dogs bay at the full moon, not making anything real out of the shadows. And under a full moon, lovers find romance that is not always for this earth!

As far back as the 6th century came the saying: "The moone is made of greene cheese." That did not refer to the color but rather to an unripened cheese. The moon's roundness made one think of a cheese when it was golden yellow, before it was put into the press to ripen.

Indian lore was to the effect that if the new moon tipped up enough to hold a powder horn on its point, the month would be a dry one. The white man said the new crescent must hold water or it would be a rainy season. Or it must hold a pail of water on its tip if it would be dry weather.

Superstitions about the moon go back to the dark ages. Nations worshipped the moon as a god. The word lunatic comes from the word luna, meaning a weak or wavering person, one who was influenced by the light of the moon and who had turned mentally. "No one should ever let moonlight shine on him as he sleeps," the old superstition said.

Killing animals for food, gathering herbs, sowing seeds, cutting wood were all supposed to be regulated by the moon. The idea persisted even to the days of the American Colonies and no doubt there are many village folk who believe such ideas now. Blood flowed differently in animals when the moon waxed and waned, herbs and all growing things were affected by this and even the sap in wood is affected. Woodsmen said

219

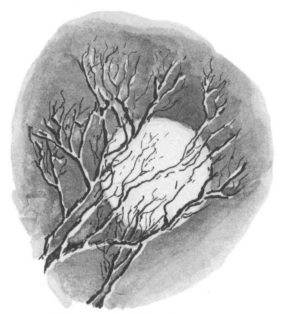

The moon in all its glory

that timber cut in the wane of the moon was more durable than that cut between the new moon and the full moon. Timber was cut before the sap began to flow back in the early spring, in February. That is the month when the sap returns and is harvested. There were no leaves to cut off the boughs and snow was deep enough to make it easy for scoots to take timber out of the forest at that time in February.

We all know from forecasts that the moon has a great influence on the weather. It causes the rise and fall of the tides, which are at their highest at full moon. If a storm comes at this time the combination makes for a most destructive storm. This has happened many times in the past on the coast. A full moon is apt to bring clouds or a storm, two days before to two days after there is apt to be a disturbance.

We have the Harvest moon in September and the Hunter's moon in October, when the moon rises at the same point for several nights and remains full for a longer time. The names were applied to those moons by the white man, when he reaped his harvest in September and found more prey to kill in October.

Horoscopes warn us not to start anything new on the day of the new moon. But following that, the period for two weeks is most auspicious for action and progress. Then things slow down again and we are cautioned to wait. Try to catch the new moon when it is a thin sickle in the West and look at it over your right shoulder. That will bring good luck.

62

OLD BRIDAL CUSTOMS FOR JUNE BRIDES

JUNE IS THE MONTH FOR BRIDES. MAY WAS ALWAYS CONSIDERED AN UN-lucky month, but June seems to offer all that could delight the heart of a young bride, with its natural beauty and balmy days.

Many years ago in the countries across the water, it was the custom to strew herbs, flowers, and rushes on the way to church as the bridal party proceeded. That custom changed to throwing rice and it is rice that is used today.

It is strange to read that the best man was at one time the man who helped capture the bride, back in the countries where brides-to-be were literally captured. That custom must have started with the beginning of marriages. Today, the best man is still an important part of every wedding ceremony.

What the bride would wear on her wedding day has always been chosen with care. At one time, every bit of her wedding apparel had to be new, even to a last pin. Any color could be chosen but green. In some sections, the bride borrowed something from a former bride. Today's homely rhyme says:

> Something old and something new,
> Something borrowed and something blue.

Many years ago, the bride-to-be sent flowers and gloves to those who were invited to the wedding. Bride-cake was even sent to friends and relatives. The wedding feast often lasted a week, with much food and wine. Among the poorer classes, guests brought contributions.

In the early years, the bride tossed a garter which would be worn by the lucky person who caught it, on her wedding day. Today, a bride tosses her bouquet to those gathered at the foot of the staircase. Catching a rose brings good luck and an early marriage.

The gifts to the bride were overly useful rather than beautiful or ornamental. A birch broom for the floor was an important gift, as was a wafer iron. The wife spent her days attending her household rather than enjoying social activities.

If a groom built a new house or put on an addition to his parents' house, the bride-to-be took pains to drive in one peg so she could say part of the house was hers. No one seems to know why a bride is carried over the threshold of her new home, but that custom still prevails.

Old bridal customs for June brides

A strange custom has come down by word of mouth and a few visible proofs exist today showing that it was followed in many sections. This is as it has been told: In the days of the early Colonists in the 18th century, a bride-to-be stepped into a closet before the marriage ceremony. She was clad only in her chemise or smock. Hanging in the closet were the bridal garments. In the door of the closet was a hole, the shape of a diamond or heart, about five inches long. The bridegroom stood outside the door to the room. The bride-to-be thrust her hand through the diamond-shaped hole and the groom took it in his. No words were spoken. This act, preliminary to the marriage, signified that the groom would not be responsible for any debts the bride-to-be had incurred; she came to him with no worldly goods and her previous life was put into the past. Then, withdrawing her hand, she dressed in her bridal garments and came forth for the legal ceremony. Because of such a ceremony the present-day mock ceremony has come to take place.

It is very seldom one sees a diamond-shaped hole in an old house. Even at that, I have found owners who did not know why such a hole had been made. One in Newfane, Vermont, another in Francestown, New Hampshire, and a third in Princeton, Massachusetts, are mute evidence of this strange custom. Sometimes it is a closet door and sometimes it is a door between two rooms, or a hall and a room. In a town not far from Worcester, the hole in the door is at the foot of the stairs, leading to the upper chambers. This would show that the bride-to-be probably dressed up in her room before ascending the stairs.

Customs may come and customs may go, but June brides go on forever.

63

OLD SAYINGS THAT SURVIVE THE YEARS

Georgie Porgie, Puddin' Pie
Kissed the girls and made them cry.
When the girls went out to play,
Georgie Porgie ran away.

I HAVE CHANTED THAT RHYME HUNDREDS OF TIMES IN MY CHILDHOOD, but never once questioned about Puddin' Pie. Now in my research work, I have found that pudding pie was a meat pie, served under a crust, the first of the making of pies.

And I found much more. "Whistle for it" and "Wet your whistle" was what we would say to someone who wanted more and could not get it. In the early days in old taverns, the large wooden tankards were made with a handle all in one piece. At the top of the handle was a whistle. This was in England. When anyone wanted his tankard filled again, he summoned an attendant by whistling, blowing on the top of the handle. That saying, "You'll have to whistle for it" or "Go whistle for it" has survived many, many centuries.

Surviving, too, for a thousand and more years is the saying, "He isn't worth his salt," The Roman soldiers were paid by salt, so doubtless at times they were found to be not worth their salt.

"Dyed in the wool" and "All wool and a yard wide" came into existence when every housewife dyed the wool that was taken from the sheep, and, after much preparation, wove it on their looms. Everything on the early looms was made a yard wide, the width of the loom.

The pot of stew was a common fare in the early days and that comes into many sayings. If it's "pot luck" you do not know what is in the pot and you would be gambling on something. If it has "gone to pot" it is lost; gone with whatever was cast into the pot. "The melting pot" is a conglomeration of things in the pot, either stew, odd bits of glass to be fused, or the like. That is also used today as an expression of the melding of races.

The Dutch and the Scotch come in for their share of attention. "If it doesn't beat the Dutch" shows that someone has gone one better than the Dutch. They were thrifty, good providers, and shrewd. A Dutch treat means sharing equally and a Dutch Uncle would be someone who would be generous and who would take care of some person.

The goose figures in some expressions. We call someone a "goose" when they are stupid and do not understand. But a goose is not dumb. They have even been used as a watch, crying out when trouble was at hand. "Gone as a goose" came from the dead goose, ready to be prepared for cooking. In Rhode Island is a town called Seekonk. That name came from the fact that there were many wild geese and gulls and their honking brought the name from Sea Honk to Seekonk.

Old sayings that serve the years

A good housewife had her house in "apple pie order." If you have never made an apple pie, you would not know how you set the slices of apple side by side, right around the rim of the crust, all in order. When the pies were set away in the larder, they were placed one upon the other or in holders one above the other, in "apple pie order." Some housewife must have described a neighbor generations ago when she said she kept her house in "apple pie order."

When it comes to personality, it is better to be nice than disagreeable. "You can catch more flies with molasses than with vinegar." You might be as "homely as a hedge fence" or "never be hung for your beauty" but try not to "bite off more than you can chew." You can be as "spry as a cricket" or "dead as a door nail" or "fit to be tied" or "not worth a hill of beans." You can escape trouble by a "hair's breadth" or be sure "it all comes out in the wash."

If you have a good memory and a good imagination, you will be sure to follow along with me as I write down these sayings. How many more do you remember?

64

OLD SAYINGS AND WEATHER OBSERVATIONS

WHAT WOULD WE DO IF WE DID NOT HAVE THE WEATHER TO HELP US in our conversation! No matter what season of the year is with us, we can always say, "Nice day, isn't it!" or "What a day!" or "did you ever see such weather!"

When I was a little girl of three, I used to ask for the daily paper and say, "I want to see weather." I put it on the floor and lay down flat on my stomach and pretended to find out about the weather. Perhaps that was the beginning of my weather observations, for I have always been sensitive to changes and have been able to predict them.

Our New England ancestors left a wealth of weather lore for us and most of it is in use today, scientifically and other wise. Those hardy folk lived in the open and with no help from mechanical devices they observed and followed Nature.

Old sayings and weather observations

From observing the sun, moon, and clouds, many sayings came into existence. "When the sun goes down as an orange ball, it is going to be hot and dry." "Red in the morning, sailors take warning, red at night, sailors' delight." "Rain before seven, clear before eleven." If it is foggy in the morning, it will clear before noon and if it clears in the night after a storm, it will rain again soon—the storm backs up. The scientific time for the weather to clear is about nine in the morning and four in the afternoon. When the sun sets Thursday, you can know the prediction for the weekend; if it sets in clouds, rain or snow will come within forty-eight hours; if it sets in a clear sky, fair weather will follow.

The Indian lore said, if the new moon was tipped enough to hold a powder horn on its point, the month would be a dry one. A ring around the moon foretells a storm and by counting the number of stars within the ring, you can reckon the number of days before a storm comes. A storm is apt to occur two days before a full moon or two days after—not always as a severe storm. I have followed this for as many years as I can remember and found there was scarcely a month that did not have a spell of bad weather near the time of the full moon. The moon effects the tides, causing an increase in height, and if a storm occurs at full moon with a high tide, it will be most severe. Our New England coastal storms have taken a heavy toll at high tides.

The moon has always had great magnetic power over man, beasts, and Nature. Timber was cut following the full moon of February. Brush was cut on the old moon of August. Soap was made on the increase of the moon or it would be thin and beef and pork animals were killed on the increase of the moon or the meat would shrink in cooking. The full moon was made for lovers and it was then that dogs bayed at the weird shadows.

The last Friday of the month, according to the old lore, predicts the weather for the following month, and many believe that the last three days of the month forecast the kind of weather to come in the following month.

If water boils away rapidly, the barometer is falling and a storm is in the air. And when smoke is beaten down from the chimney, the barometer is falling. Some say that when leaves are turned over by wind, the falling barometer foretells a storm. Birds and animals sense storms and approaching changes. When birds swoop in circles toward the ground, they are after bugs driven down before a coming storm. The migration of birds forecasts the approaching change in seasons, whether they be early or late. When cows lie down in the morning, farmers say it is going to rain. An early visit from a skunk in spring is a sign of the breaking up of winter. By the thickness of animals' fur, the kind of winter is foretold, since Nature provides this protection. Some say if a chipmunk carries his tail out straight, it predicts a hard winter. Ordinarily, the tail is standing straight in the air.

Candlemas Day, on the second of February, has become an event. Everyone watches to check the behavior of the groundhog. If he sees his shadow, he returns for six more weeks of hibernation, at the end of which time, spring will arrive.

Saint Swithin, an English builder of churches, requested that he be buried by a roadside where the public passed. In the year 923, his body was exhumed in order for it to be placed in a cathedral. Torrents of rain came from the heavens for forty days; this was taken as a protest by the people. From this came Saint Swithin's Day, the 15th of July, which gives the forecast of weather for forty days.

Weathercocks were mounted on every barn in the old days, to tell the direction of the wind. Today, few are seen. If there is no vane to see to find the direction of the wind, moisten a forefinger and raise it aloft, and gauge the direction of the wind against it. A South wind in summer means fair weather; if it shifts toward the East it brings rain. West winds bring fair weather all the year around. If, when a storm clears, the wind blows cold from the North, the storm has backed up and will come again. A Northeast wind brings a storm of three days, while a Sou'easter is not of long duration. A perfectly beautiful, clear day, with a sharp blue sky, is called a "weather breeder." It foretells a storm in the offing.

Man has built all of his sciences upon observations. Some of these are recorded while others stand as common sayings.

65

BLAME IT ON THE MOON IF YOU LACK AMBITION

IN ANCIENT TIMES, THE MOON WAS AN OBJECT OF WORSHIP. IT WAS supposed to have much influence on man and beast as well as Nature. The time for killing animals for food, the time for sowing seeds, for cutting herbs, for cutting timber was all regulated by the phases of the moon. Loss and disappointments would be incurred if the proper phase of the moon was not observed. The moon even governed the time for taking medicine or curing diseases. The words lunatic and moonstruck come from the influence of the moon.

The new moon was the time for beginning new ventures. As the moon increased, so did the powers of man and beast. The full moon was the height of that power. As the moon decreased in size and became the "old moon," inactivity followed; both mental and physical powers decreased.

In the days of our ancestors, the same knowledge prevailed, coming from observations. Such jobs as cutting timber, killing animals, and making candles or soap were done on the increase of the moon. Timber cut before the full moon was found to be more sound than that cut after the moon had begun to wane, because the moon affected the flow of the sap.

We are all effected by the weather. When it is fair, clear, and cold, we have a feeling of strength and ambition. When it is sultry, damp, and stormy with East winds, we settle into a depression that we cannot shake. We are restless, disturbed, and have no ambition. Even the gentle South winds take away our energy.

Today, psychologists are telling us to watch ourselves for reactions at the time of the various phases of the moon. Emotionally and physically, we feel the pull of the moon as it moves through its orbit. We think more easily, we accomplish things more quickly with less effort. After the peak is reached, we feel a let-down. It is then that we have little ambition; we

Blame it on the moon if you lack ambition

do not want to make any effort and we do only routine work. Our creative ability lies dormant.

Twenty-five years ago, there appeared one of Pitkin's books, *More Power to You*. Someone gave me a copy and I credit that book for a change that came into my ways of living. Pitkin described so well our ups and downs, saying that each person has them of certain duration and intensity. He says to watch the waves and make mental notes of the length, work hard on the "up" waves and create as much as possible. When the "down" wave comes, "don't kick," he says. Plan for the loss of energy and ambition by accepting it and thinking it cannot last. Have some activity ready that does not take the greatest amount of power and energy and tide over the spell until the "up" wave comes again.

If we understand ourselves as controlled by the moon's phases and by the weather, we can gain both emotionally and physically.

66

WISHFUL THINKING CAN BE FUN

Star bright, star light,
First star I've seen tonight;
Wish I may, wish I might
Have the wish I wish tonight.

Four posts upon my bed,
Two posts above my head;
Matthew, Mark, Luke and John,
Bless the bed I lay upon;
Matthew, John, Luke and Mark,
Grant my wish and keep it dark.

HOW LONG SINCE YOU HAVE SAID THAT RHYME WHEN YOUR EYES FELL upon the first star after sunset? Even though you have gone beyond the wishing stage, it is a wonderful feeling to gaze up into the heavens and say that little rhyme. Try it some night and wish for something close to your heart. Psychologists say if we concentrate on something we want, it can be ours.

And there is the wish-bone, the breast bone of chickens, turkeys, and all birds; it comes in the shape of a fork with a flat head. In our house this bone is never thrown away. The carcass of the chicken or turkey goes into soup and the wishbone goes on top of the stove to dry. When it is thoroughly dry, two of us wish, each taking a tip end. Then we make a wish, count three, and pull. The one who gets the head or the longer piece has his wish granted. Does that sound silly? It never was that bad.

Did you ever start to say something at the same time someone else said it? If that happened, you would link your little fingers together, make a wish, place the two thumbs together and say, "thumbs!" Then one of you would ask, "What goes up the chimney?" The other answered, "smoke." That clinched the wish and both of you would have it granted, in some future time.

We never saw a daisy without wanting to pick off the petals, one at a time and say, "He loves me, he loves me not" until we came to the end. Perhaps he loved us and perhaps he did not! And then we used to find out whom we were going to marry by saying a rhyme on the buttons on our dress:

> Rich man, poor man, beggar man, thief,
> Doctor, lawyer, merchant, chief.

We repeated this until all the buttons on all our clothes were counted and we had found out who our future lover would be.

Wishful thinking can be fun

Remember the load of hay that went down the road? Hay was not bundled in the old days but was pitched onto a hay wagon, with the driver and others atop it all. How many times we children rode in the hay as it was being pitched up in the fields and then rode on top of the load to the barn! When a load of hay passed us if we were walking or driving, we wished on it and turned away. If by chance our eye caught it again, we lost our wish. We were very careful not to look back! If the hay wagon was drawn by a white horse, that brought our wish for sure. A load of empty barrels filled the same purpose. Both hay and barrels were common sights long ago. Today, modern methods have deprived us of those wonderful chances to make a wish.

> See a pin, pick it up.
> All that day, you'll have good luck.

> See a pin and let it lay,
> You'll have bad luck all the day.

A slanting pin means a ride, the point bad luck, and the head good luck. Stick a pin in wood and the wish is sure to come true.

It is a wonderful feeling to see the new moon, a faint sickle, and make a wish. See it over the right shoulder and you have good luck; over the left shoulder, bad luck; straight ahead, hard work; and through a window, bad luck. Be sure to turn your right shoulder when you look for the new moon in the evening sky.

Wishful thinking? It never seemed to be. Perhaps if we put ourselves back in those days and wish once in a while, it might help as we go along in these hard days.

PART VI
THROUGH FIELDS, WOODS AND TOWN

67

THE TIN PEDDLER AND OTHERS

WHENEVER A TIN PEDDLER'S CART IS MENTIONED, THERE IS ALWAYS someone who says, "Why, I remember one when I was a girl!" The peddler and his cart did not entirely disappear until about 1890 or 1900. Many of the older generation remember them well and can describe them as if it were yesterday that these carts were on the road.

The peddler's cart was long and painted red, with many compartments and racks. The earliest ones had wooden axles and wood springs and leather fastenings. Nearly always the cart was made with a shaft for two horses, for the day's journey was a hard one. Often it was a journey of several months.

The driver's seat was high with a box compartment on either side. The dasher was high and curved as graceful as a swan's neck. The floor-board lifted and there was a shallow compartment underneath. The box-like compartments at either end of the driver's seat were a foot high and 25 inches long, with a door that dropped down on leather hinges. Below each one was another compartment that went in under the driver's seat, opening with a door on leather hinges.

In the main body of the wagon was one large compartment. A long door on either side lifted with a latch. Inside was a deep cavity across which was a shelf on tracks. The shelf could be moved or slid so it could be reached on either side of the cart. Behind the driver's seat, on top of the cavity, was a floor with a railing around it. Large, heavy pieces of tin-ware were carried here, while in the cavity, on the sliding shelf and in other compartments, notions and small wares were carried.

At the back of the wagon was a slatted rack that dropped down, held by straps on either side. Here was another place for bulky things and, on the return trip, bags of rags and all sorts of things taken in trade. Scales hung by the side to weigh those things and racks for brooms were near this back part.

Tin peddler

Before the days of the peddler's cart, peddlers went on foot, carrying two tin trunks, slung over their shoulders with webbing harness or leather straps. They were called "pack peddlers." The things peddled from those trunks were called Yankee notions, such as pins, needles, hooks and eyes, scissors, razors, combs, brushes, buttons, spoons, cotton goods, and laces by the yard and perfumes.

When the peddler went on his trips in a cart, he added books, straw hats, shoes, brooms, jackknives, woodenware, snuff boxes, tobacco, and reading spectacles. In the beginning of the 19th century, the peddler took no money, but made his sales by bartering. In exchange he took linen rags, wool, skins with the wool left on and skins with the wool off, hog bristles, pelts, old and worn-out articles of copper, brass, and pewter. And wood ashes were valuable in trade for they went to soap manufacturers who made lye from them for their soap. Fat and grease were taken, too, for the soap and candle establishments. The peddler was the go-between for the housewife's supply of rags, ashes, and grease.

It was the New England youths who took to the road. They had the Yankee characteristics of being quick-witted, industrious, and adventurous. They were persuasive and could easily strike a bargain.

Tinsmiths began to manufacture their wares as early as 1786. Long before the Civil War, tin was a necessary commodity, replacing wooden and iron utensils. Sheets of tin were imported from England before any tin mines were found in this country. The sheets were $11\frac{7}{8}$ by 9 inches and $18\frac{3}{8}$ by $11\frac{3}{8}$ inches and were packed in wooden boxes, made of elm, which was tough, strong, and flexible enough to take nails without split-ting. Tinware was a joy to the housewife and gave new life to the drab kitchens. It was the tinsmith who supplied the peddler and the two worked in close cooperation with each other. The peddler would load his cart at a tinsmith's shop for a long trip South, West, or to Canada, sell out completely, load up again with another tinsmith in a far distant town, and make a return trip.

Many large stores today began their existence from a tin peddler's cart. Among the many men who made their life's vocation with tinware were Bronson Alcott, John Boynton and Jonas G. Clark, not counting other men of prominence, like R. H. Macy of New York, who had their first experiences of life by peddling. Bronson Alcott of Concord fame, born in 1799 and living a span of 89 years, became a peddler against the wishes of his parents, who had chosen a college career for him. He went to New Jersey on his first trip and made as much as 2200 per cent profit, and could give glowing accounts on his return. Starting a second trip, he took a younger brother. Things went hard. The brother returned home. Bronson had many disappointments. He came home with no cash, but with many experiences which he had written in a diary from day to day, sitting by the roadside.

John Boynton was born in Mason, New Hampshire, in 1791. He worked on his father's farm. In 1821, the family moved to New Ipswich, New Hampshire, to continue farming. In 1825, John moved to Templeton, Massachusetts, and started a tin shop and a Japanning shop, where trays were Japanned, which was a special finishing process. Both of these shops are still standing on the Hubbardston road; one is used as a Grange Hall.

By 1845, John made enough tinware to supply 27 carts; the peddlers would go on day trips. David Whitcomb, a young man of the town, went to work without pay with John. For an entire year, he had to work with-out pay to prove his worth. Then he was given $100 and a vest pattern, the last being cloth for a vest, which in those days was the showpiece of a man's costume.

John Boynton retired in 1846. He realized the need of education for young men, especially in the field of mechanics. So he gave his money for a school that was to be called Worcester Polytechnic Institute. This school was founded in 1867 and the hall and the street on which the grounds faced carry the name of Boynton.

Jonas G. Clark was born in Hubbardston, Massachusetts, in 1800. He attended the district school and worked on his father's farm. At the age of 16, he became an apprentice in a carriage shop there in town. On learning the trade, he established his own carriage shop. He exchanged the carriages and wagons he had made for hard wood supplied by the farmers. From this wood he made chairs, which he sold in Boston. When tin utensils were beginning to be popular, Jonas was attracted by their popularity—they were a cheap and attractive ware. He never became a tin peddler but set up stores in Lowell and Milford, Massachusetts, where he sold tinware. Of a restless nature, he again turned to shipping furniture and other goods to California. He even went to that state. With the money he had made in his various trades, he bought real estate there and in New York, which he sold at a profit of 65 per cent. His health gave out and he came back East. He, too, realized the need of education for young men, and in 1887 he founded Clark University in Worcester, Massachusetts. When he died in 1900, a sum of money was left for Clark College, a school separate from the University.

Such is the history of the three young men who were born not far from Worcester, who lived at the time of the beginning of tinware and the tin cart. Many more men from all over New England took to the road. It was said that in Maine more men graduated from the tin cart than from Bates College and that their education and experiences were more complete.

It was a colorful era, that of the tin peddler and his cart. The few carts that have survived are now preserved in Museums and the memories will live in the minds of the older generations.

Today, the man who rings the back door bell does not call himself a peddler. He is a "salesman." How often he brings you to the front door, vexing you beyond words! No matter whether it be a magazine, brushes, or buns that he carries, he is a salesman.

We see many types of traveling peddlers and salesmen on the streets today, such as the Bookmobile of the Public Library, the Canteen that carries food, the hot dog truck, the popcorn vender and the ice cream man. All of these are necessities of a city and a form of salesmanship. The Bookmobile and the Canteen belong to a class by themselves and to those might be added the traveling piano that journeys through small towns out West where children who are denied music have the opportunity to learn the art of playing and singing.

It might seem a long ways back to some, but to me it is just yesterday when the town had more peddlers than you could count on the fingers of both your hands. I remember the thrill of having the peddlers stop at the back door and I stood by Mother's side as she chose her wares. One of the peddlers was Aunt Betsy, the old bluing woman. She was nearly blind, with one eye out of focus, had only a few teeth, was very deaf, and was clad in voluminous skirts touching the ground, and an old shawl pinned around her thin shoulders, topped by a small bonnet. She carried an old cane. She claimed she had been a slave at the time of the Civil War, and by her looks the story was believable.

Mother always bought a bottle of Aunt Betsy's home-made bluing even though there might be a bottle or two on the shelf in the pantry. She carried the bottles in an old carpet bag. She always asked for a drink of water, for walking tired her. Sometimes Mother would give her a cup of coffee. Then Aunt Betsy would sit on the top step of the back piazza and drink and rest. "Jes' to rest ma weary bones. I'se more'n a hundre' years ole." She talked a good deal as she sat there but you did not attempt any conversation with her, letting her ramble on. What with her eyes rolling around and her almost toothless mouth and the tapping of her cane on a lower step as she talked, I was a bit frightened and yet I wanted to watch her. It was quite some time before she was rested and before she could lift herself up onto her feet and be off. The thud of her cane beat out each step as she went down the long board walk to the street, still talking to herself.

The man with the spools of sewing silk came twice a year. He had only one arm and was very deaf. He carried his boxes of colored spools in a small bag slung over his shoulder and he would come into the dining room and lay his bag on the table. Such boxes, of gorgeous colors: real silk made by Clark, Corticelli, and Heminway, 100 yards at 5 cents a spool! I believe we still have some of those spools of colored silk. The sewing man did not tarry, for he was very shy.

There was a man who came regularly to our back door who had a wooden bucket of horseradish. His bucket had a cover and he scooped out the amount you wanted with a tin scoop, putting it into a dish you brought out from the pantry. Father liked horseradish, but I was never interested in watching the peddler or the stuff he sold. In my collection of wooden pails and buckets today, who knows but what I might have one such bucket that carried horseradish!

The scissors grinder had a bell attached to his push-wagon, so you always knew when he was in the neighborhood. He did a thriving business for it seemed as if every one of the womenfolks did their own sewing and scissors always needed to be kept sharp. I used to go out in the back yard and watch him work; the sparks would fly as the metal went over the grindstone. There was a small seat that dropped down and he sat as he worked. A collection of those two-wheeled vehicles of the scissors grinder should be in some museum, but I guess those push-wagons went the way of the one-horse shay!

The hokey-pokey ice cream man used to go through the streets ringing his bell and selling his stuff. I do not remember that I was allowed to buy hokey-pokey ice cream, for we had an ice cream freezer and we had delicious ice cream and lemon sherbert, which was enough for us. And in the winter, we took a dish full of clean snow, poured a little vanilla onto it, sweetened it, and called it ice cream. Was it a treat after a nice snow-storm! So I watched the hokey-pokey man pass by with no longings.

More peddlers could be described, in those days of the Gay Nineties. We hardly have a chance to miss them today, for where there used to be one peddler of yesterday, there are a dozen salesmen today, of different kinds and of different importance.

68

IT'S TIME TO TAP AGAIN

THE OTHER DAY I DREW MY CAR UP TO THE CURB TO PARK AND DO AN errand. A few drops splashed on my windshield and knowing it was not a shower of rain, I said aloud, "The sap is running again."

It is the last of February when the sap begins to flow back in the trees. There are visible signs of it in the maple trees when tiny icicles of sap form after a frosty, cold night. We have a maple tree at the back of our house, and many times I have seen squirrels break off the little icicles and feast on them with relish.

To be a successful season for sap gathering, beginning the last of February and on into March, there must be warm, sunny days and cold, frosty nights. This causes the sap to rise and flow, recede and flow more actively each day.

In the early days, every family had a maple grove, both for the wood from the trees and for the sap, giving the family a substantial income. Sugar, sugar-molasses, and syrup were obtained for the table and often for bartering. The Indians taught the white man how to tap the trees. They used what Nature had to offer in the way of a stone spout. After gouging out a hole they drove in the spout. A wooden trough made from a hollowed-out log lay on the ground, into which the sap ran. The white man used a spout, or spile as it was called, made from a foot-long sumac twig with the pith burned out. Under the spile, a wooden bucket with one handle was placed to catch the dripping sap. That particular bucket tapered toward the top, the better to hold the liquid. It had one protruding stave, cut short, with a hole in the end, by which it hung on the spile. A bucket with one short arm was distinctly a sap bucket. When tin came into use, the wooden spile changed to one of tin made with a lip near the end onto which the bucket hung.

Carrying buckets had two protruding staves or ears with holes in them. A stick was thrust through the holes to enable them to be carried.

243

It's time to tap again

With a shoulder yoke, a man could easily carry two buckets without spilling, the weight taken by the yoke on his shoulders. The buckets were
emptied into big tubs that stood waiting on a low platform on runners.
This was called a scoot and was drawn by two oxen into the grove. When
the tubs were full, they were taken to the sugar house. Children often
helped in this work, joining in the fun of watching the buckets fill. Tin
pails took the place of the staved wooden buckets, when tin came onto
the market.

The sugar house was in the grove with perhaps a shack or two nearby.
In the house was a brick foundation for a fire on which four or five kettles
could be placed to hold the boiling syrup. The fire was not allowed to
go out and had to be fed for three successive days and nights, the time
it took to boil down the sap. Often it took another full day. Some of the
family slept in the shacks in order to tend the fires.

The first run of sap was made into cakes. In the beginning, there were
wooden box molds, with partitions which could be taken out after the
sugar had hardened. A design was on the bottom of each square, for
decoration. Tin came in due time and then came tin molds, of fancy shapes
such as hearts, flowers, and figures. The cakes were wrapped and packed
in tubs to be taken to market later in the year.

The second run of sap made a darker syrup. This was poured into
large tubs and stored in the attic. As the sugar set, a sugar molasses
formed. The bung hole was plugged with a twist of straw as a stopper,

to let in the air and keep out the ants. The sugar molasses was drawn off as it was needed in cooking or for buckwheat cakes. This was all that was known before molasses from the sugar cane found its way to the table and the soft sugar was used before white sugar was known.

When the last of the sugar had been made into cakes or poured into tubs, the families from near and far came to the camp for a sugaring-off party. Singing and playing games and pouring syrup on snow made an evening of gaiety, indelibly imprinted on the minds of young and old. With the moon shinging on the snow, the sharply outlined shadows, and the light of the fires, it was a picture long to remember.

Today, sap gathering has become a tremendous business, with one state vying with another. As we drive through country towns in March, we often see pails hanging on maple trees that are scattered here and there. We know that some boy or man wants whatever sap he can gather to make into syrup. Maple sugar and maple syrup has always been a delicacy.

When spring is on its way, the sap begins to run again.

69

THERE WERE FEW COMFORTS
IN THE OLD CHURCHES

UP IN THE HISTORICAL SOCIETY IN THE LITTLE TOWN OF NEW BRAINTREE, not far from Worcester, I found an odd relic, which proved to be an arm rest once used in a pew in church. I brought it home and photographed it.

It was made by Samuel Harrington for his wife Saphrona Converse, whom he married September 19, 1820, the label read. It has an upright part which is a turned standard, a rest across the top and a base at the bottom. The top is padded with homespun linen over lamb's wool, edged with a colored gimp fastened with brass tacks. The entire piece stands 15 inches high.

It must have been a relief to rest one's arm on such a contrivance, when sitting bolt upright in a straightback pew! I have such a piece in my museum but had never been quite sure what it was. Mine has no padding. I have seen several such pieces with no padding, which make me realize how thoughtful Samuel Harrington was when he put on padding.

The days of the old churches seem far back in history—the days of little comforts. The pews had narrow, wooden seats with high, straight backs. Each pew had a small door that fastened with a wooden button. The families brought their own footstoves to make the cold more durable and the little doors helped keep in the heat. Even when stoves appeared in 1734, footstoves were still used for the extra heat. Sometimes the women carried in their muffs a small cake of soapstone that had been heated and made warm to a certain degree.

People were seated in church according to the amount of money they gave and according to their rank in town. Important townspeople were up front and the rest were graded toward the back. When stoves appeared, the grading began from the heat, down to the back of the church where no heat circulated.

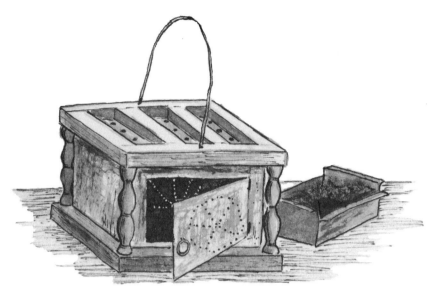

There were few comforts in the old churches

Although footstoves burning charcoal were long enough to accommodate two or three people, other methods were resorted to. It has been recorded that men would bring dogs so that they might rest their feet on their warm bodies. This was prohibited in short order and no dog was allowed in church.

Among the papers in our old secretary is a deed given to my grandfather, Rufus Gould, for a pew in the town of Barre, just north of Worcester. It states that he paid the sum of $45 for a certain pew, "To have and to hold the same to the said Gould, his heirs and Assigns, to his and their use and behoof forever with all privileges and appurtenances thereof belonging."

Few were the comforts in those times of worshipping in cold churches. A long ride in open sleighs, a long service lasting morning and afternoon, and a long ride home. Our ancestors were hardy.

70

GOING TO SABBATH MEETING

OUR ANCESTORS MUST HAVE BEEN A HARDY LOT TO HAVE WITHSTOOD THE ordeal of going to Sabbath meeting. Whether it was in the dead of winter, or heat of summer, the day-long service was a test of endurance.

Nearly all of the Meeting Houses were built on a hill. This was so the white church with its towering steeple might be a guide for travelers, or a landmark for sailors as they approached the coast. Another reason a hill was chosen for a church was to give the men a vantage point to watch for marauding Indians. In some sections, the men carried guns on the Sabbath until as late as 1746.

The families were scattered over the countryside and it was often a long ride to the Meeting House. The church in the early days was small, with boxed-in pews, a high pulpit at one end, and a small organ in the gallery at the other, around which sat the choir. The singers were thus behind the congregation so they would not distract those in the meeting.

Records tell of seven different divisions in seating the people. They were seated by rank and by the amount they had given to support the church. Those of important station in the village and those who gave generously were seated near the front. The tapering off reached the back of the church to just plain folks. The unmarried men were on one side and the unmarried women on the other side, with the boys of the village sitting on the steps of the pulpit and of the gallery. Nothing is said of the little girls so it is supposed that they sat with their parents and needed no discipline.

At first, the seats in the Meeting House were benches, with a single board for the back. Then came pews, spelled "pues" in those days, with high walls and narrow seats that were hinged to the back of the pew. The seats shut up when the people stood and one can well imagine the noise caused by a gathering of people standing up and sitting down. Each pew was shut in with a small door on hinges that fastened with a swivel button.

The long Sabbath service included prayers, Scripture reading, and singing. Prayers more often than not were more than an hour long. At noon came the recess when the families gathered outside, sometimes in a nearby Tavern or in a Fire Room which was in a section of the shed for the horses. That room was purposely built for such gatherings and it had a fireplace. This noontime recess was the lunch hour. The families had brought food to sustain themselves for a second ordeal in the afternoon. The routine of the afternoon was similar to the morning; prayers, exhortations, and Scripture reading. The fiery, destructive parts of the Bible were stressed and everyone, even down to the children, was impressed by the wickedness of sin.

An important man during the church service was the tithing man. He was elected annually and his duty was to preserve order in the church and to make any complaint of disorderly conduct. He had to enforce the observance of the Sabbath outside the church as well. During the service, he carried a stick that had knobs on one end and a fox tail or a hare's foot on the other. The knobs were to punish unruly boys after the service. But the fox tail was the end that was used the most. Because of the long, monotonous service, most people had to make an effort to keep awake. If anyone was seen to nod, he was immediately touched with the

Going to the Sabbath meeting

fox tail and made alert again—perhaps to fall asleep more than once thereafter.

Caraway seed was supposed to help anyone keep awake and the women often wore a bouquet of flowers with this seed in it. The church was stifling hot in summer and freezing cold in winter.

Stoves did not appear in churches until 1734. Boston had a stove in the First Church in 1773 and in the Old South Church in 1783. Then the seating of the congregation was arranged according to the heat from the stove; those of high rank and those giving the most generous sum of money having the most heat and those of lesser importance farther away with no heat. Both places could be uncomfortable.

So until stoves were put into churches, the congregation sat through the services in freezing temperatures. It was then that foot stoves were created and the little warmth they afforded was just a little better than no heat at all. The stoves held a tin cup filled with charcoal or live embers.

An all-wooden foot stove in my collection came from Salem and appears very early; it is the work of some man who could handle the plane and gimlet. The door slides up in grooves. All four sides and the top have holes so any gasses might escape and the fire could have a draft. The cup for the charcoal has a sheet of tin under it and a second is fastened to the floor. This type of foot stove possibly came first, before tin was available.

The first foot stoves were made entirely of tin. A wire handle was fastened to the side edges of the top, and the door had wire hinges and a cotter pin for a latch. Following that came a similar tin stove set into a wooden frame, with four posts, slats across the top, and a solid bottom. The handle of that was fastened to the wooden frame. All of the tin foot stoves had holes in the four sides and top, pierced with a nail. There seem to be patterns that the worker followed, all free hand; a circle of holes surrounding a heart, hearts pierced in a circle of stars, and other hit-or-miss patterns. Hearts stood for love and stars signified religion. These foot stoves were made in three different sizes, for one person, two, and three. They were made in oval and round shapes as well as the common square one. The pans inside the long ones were made to fit the size of the stove, to hold more or less charcoal.

An unusual wooden foot stove appeared in 1865, a combination of stove and lantern. It has three glass windows at one end and a slanting incline at the other, on which the feet rested. It stands about ten inches high. Inside is a square, thin tin lamp with two burners. This was held in place by fitting into two slots which held it secure, free from causing a fire. This lantern foot stove could be carried to the Meeting House or to the Singing School and when returning home in the dark, the lantern could light the way. It has a label on it which reads:

Patented August 15 1865
Feet Warmer
Lantern and Foot-stool
Manufactured by
Otis H. Weed and Company
No 31 Brattle Street Boston
Directions: Use sperm oil or lard oil.
Do not allow the blaze to reach the radiator.

A similar combination stove and lantern is made entirely of tin, with three windows and side vents for air. This is in a private museum.

One of the last foot stoves to disappear from use in churches was that of tin, shaped like a long and narrow pillow and covered with ingrain carpeting. A cord on the top served as a handle by which it was carried. A long drawer holds a long cake of compressed charcoal. The handle of the drawer is made in the shape of a large star and there is a row of stars around both ends, following the curved shape of the ends. An original box of charcoal cakes came to me in an odd lot of things I bought at an auction. The name *Lehman* is stamped on each cake. I learned much later what the cakes were for, after I had begun a collection of foot stoves.

The foot stoves were filled at home, taken in the sleigh, and then carried into the church. This might explain why the pews had high walls and small doors with swivel buttons, so whatever heat came from the stoves might keep the family more comfortable.

At noontime, the duty of refilling the stoves was given to one special boy and he never skipped a single one. A friend of our family, back two generations, once served in such a capacity for a winter. If any stoves were left in the pews after the meeting, the sexton took them home for safe keeping and when the owners came to claim them, a fine was paid for negligence. Single foot stoves were for the women, while double and triple sizes provided heat for the family. Alice Morse Earle says that if a man had no stove to share, he brought a dog to service so that he might rest his feet on its warm body. That brought about a law that no dogs be allowed in church.

A woman often brought a hot potato in her muff, says one author, to help keep her hands warm. In my collection are several pieces of soapstone, one being the size of a small book, which was used to hold in a muff. Another piece of soapstone is in a slatted holder which could have been taken to church, carried by a wire handle. And one unusual piece has the name of the owner cut into it, so he might claim it if it ever went abroad. These stones are about eight inches by seven inches and they have a wire handle sprung into the stone by which they were carried. They were first heated in the fire, and at noontime recess they were heated again.

Light in the Meeting House was from the feeble rays of candles in sconces and candlesticks. Such sconces were hung around the gallery and by the pulpit and organ. A pair in my collection came from the Allen Evangelical Church in Dedham, Massachusetts, and hung there as late as 1820.

Chandeliers of tin, wood, and iron hung from the ceilings, first using candles for light and then later whale oil in glass cups. These finally changed to glass lamps burning kerosene.

When anyone begins to collect any definite thing, he is bound to find many unusual pieces. In my collection is a candle holder that a man made for his own pew. It is a small block of wood, about three inches square and two inches wide. The candle rests in a hole on the top. Running up the back and above the top is a wire that curves like a wide hook. This was made to hang on the back of the pew ahead of the family, to furnish a light, however feeble. Because those old pews slanted from the top to the bottom, the little holder has two pegs near the bottom at the back to hold the block upright. It is impossible to date such a rare piece but according to my checking of the records of that family, some ancestor made it more than 100 years ago, around 1850.

Today, we thrill at the sight of those foot stoves and warmers, at the sconces, arm rests, and other things that gave comfort in the old Meeting Houses of long ago. We collect them and learn of them. But it is hard to realize the physical discomforts that existed in the days of our ancestors. They were hardy.

71

THE DAY OF THE COUNTRY ROAD IS GONE

IT DOESN'T SEEM TOO LONG AGO THAT WE WERE DRIVING OVER COUNTRY roads. Twenty and thirty years ago, we used to "go to ride"; we were not always "going places." Somehow, we had more leisure and the cars of those years were not designed for anything higher than a moderate speed and our minds were not pitched to a high tension.

Each season of the year found us riding along country roads and exclaiming over the beauties of Nature. In the spring we would spy a Lady Slipper growing in a damp place. We would stop to pick real Solomon seal and violets. We would climb over a stone wall and pick laurel; deep pink. Later, we picked purple asters and daisies, ox-eyed or white. Goldenrod seemed to come before we realized that summer was drawing to a close.

On hot days we would take the country roads to be cool and often stop at a farm house to buy vegetables or eggs. In the fall, it was peaches, apples, and grapes that we found on stands in front of outlying farms. And corn! Right from the stalks.

In the winter, we found ourselves longing for those roads, where we could see the beauty of the snow and ice in fields and by streams. No artist could reproduce the glow of the twilight on the pure snow and the shadows from the setting sun. These were idelibly impressed upon our minds as we rode in our open car at 25 miles an hour. We would often take our flexible flyer and go out into the country and coast down some steep hill or slide over the crusts in an open field.

My favorite ride then was back of Shrewsbury, Northboro, and Old Boylston, outlying towns near Worcester. One day, I drove around the Town Hall in Shrewsbury, and coming to a fork in the road I stopped to wonder which road I should take. A native was sauntering by and I called to him. "That road goes to Boylston," he said, pointing to the left, "and that road don't go nowhere!" I took the "nowhere" road and that proved to be my introduction to new and wonderful country.

At another time, I was not sure of my direction. I stopped at a farm house. I went around to the back door, for that is where you will find a beaten path. Or maybe it is a side door leading from the barn where deep tracks have been made. The front door always seems to hide behind grasses and shrubs. When I rapped, a pleasant lady came to the screen door and as I stood on the big doorstone, the odor of baking wafted to me. The housewife told me where I was and then invited me in for some cookies. She sent some to my friend in the car.

Another time, I was alone. I stopped for eggs at an "egg" sign and went around to the side door. A most smiling housewife told me to come in. It was Saturday afternoon and cleaning day. "I'm in my stocking feet because it rests me when I am tired." She had just sat down to her afternoon cup of coffee and on the table was a big round cake with white frosting. Her urgent invitation to share her coffee and her cake was accepted and then to crown the pleasant stop, I was given a large piece of cake to take home to my mother.

That was not the first nor the last time I sat in on a coffee hour and had coffee with thick cream and a bun or cake. Sharing seems to be inborn in those busy farmer's wives.

I make friends when I go out into the open country. I go into the gardens and cut my own asparagus, pull beets and carrots, and pick ears

The day of the country road is gone

of corn from the stalks. The farmer folks teach me what is good and what to look for. In the fall, I know orchards where a busy housewife will take me out to the trees and help me pick my own apples. It has well been said that, "he who travels alone, finds the most happiness."

Today, the country road is fast disappearing. The cars are sleek and closed and built for speed. And there is no more "hill and dale." The town officers are straightening curves and cutting down hills to eliminate accidents and to increase speed. Such a pity! Those abandoned curves and empty farm houses tucked away down by the road are signs of modern life, of speed and tension.

The super roads have three and four lanes, stretching for miles and miles, perfectly constructed and posted. Arteries are being ruthlessly cut through the cities and toll roads are taking away homes and farms so that the automobile may proceed. The new cars are built to travel faster and faster, "going places!"

I like to think that friendly country roads can still be found. And I shall always have memories of friends I made as I leisurely stopped at side doors.

72

WHEN MAIL WENT BY HORSE

THE QUESTION OF POSTAL RATES HAS LONG BEEN AN IMPORTANT MATTER. Perhaps we do not appreciate the privilege we have of the rapid and safe handling of mail. Perhaps we do not appreciate the delivery of mail by air, of special delivery and of parcel post delivery of packages both large and small.

The word "post" has many meanings. It comes from the French word "poste" meaning the place where horses were kept. Then the word came to describe a traveler or courier who carried letters, messages, or parcels on horseback. "Post" can mean a station for keeping horses for relay traveling or a building for postal business. Our word "posthaste" is derived from the fact that the post, the courier, was supposed to ride with haste.

Alice Morse Earle describes the post as being the mail carrier who went on horseback. One of his duties was to assist any person who cared to make the journey with him. It was in 1704 that the schoolmistress Madam Knights made her famous journey from Boston to New York, the first woman to make the trip, accompanied by the post. Her diary is an important bit of history.

The first regular mail carried by the post on horseback from New York to Boston was begun on January 1, 1673. The post carried two traveling bags, called portmanteaus, one either side of the horse. He took letters and parcels. He changed his horse but once, in Hartford.

The post had to report the condition of all roads and ferries and fords. When he arrived at his destination, he laid his mail on the table at an inn and anyone expecting a letter would be there to claim it. Often letters remained on the table or bar for days and any and all could look them over and know who was hearing from whom. The postal rates were high.

Some posts in certain sections went on foot and did not begin the journey until they had enough letters to pay the expense of the trip. These foot posts had a tough time of it, crossing ponds and streams on their skates in winter and making many roundabout routes in summer. Foot posts carried mail as late as 1730, one route being from New York to Albany.

Many post riders pursued much more than the business of carrying letters. They collected postage money for themselves, they transferred money to their advantage, they returned horses and even fetched oxen to an owner. It is on record that an old postrider knitted mittens and stockings as he slowly jogged along on his horse.

Horseback riding brought about horse blocks in front of nearly every house. One such block can be seen at Fruitlands in Harvard, Massachusetts, in front of the Shaker House. They are wooden steps.

It was Benjamin Franklin who set milestones by the side of the road to measure the distance from one town to another, to help postal rates. On the postroad—so named because it was the road over which the post was carried from Boston to Philadelphia—milestones were located the entire way. A few of them can still be seen.

Franklin rode in his chaise, which had an adjustable device attached to it, known as a cyclometer. It measured the miles as he traveled. When he had ridden a certain number of miles, he stopped, and from a cart which went alongside his chaise, a stone was dropped. Next came men from the town who set the stone into place by the side of the road. These milestones enabled the post carriers to know how far they were traveling and how much to charge for each letter.

When the mail went by horse

In my Century Book of Facts, I found the following rates for letters: Before 1854, the postal rate on letters varied from six cents for carrying a distance of 30 miles to 25 cents for 400 miles. It was reduced that same year to five cents a distance for 300 miles or less and ten cents for any distance beyond that.

In 1851, the rate was three cents for every half ounce for 3000 miles and six cents for over that distance. In 1863, the postage was again reduced to two cents for half an ounce for letters sent less than 3000 miles and in 1885, to two cents an ounce. This last rate remained until the change came in July 6, 1932, making it three cents an ounce. Then in August, 1958, the rates again moved up to four cents an ounce. In 1966 they were raised to five cents an ounce, and in 1968 to six cents.

The first stamp was authorized by Congress on March 3, 1847. There was then a five-cent stamp and a ten-cent stamp.

Letters arriving in this country from across the water at the port of Boston were delivered on board ship. Those that were not called for were taken to a coffee house near the wharf where they were spread out on a table to await their owners. The coffee-houses grew into common use and they became the first post offices.

Every small town en route from one principal city to another had a post office. Generally it was in an inn but often the owner of a private house undertook the position. My elderly friend from "Down East," who told me many stories of her early life, said her father had the post office in his home and she as a little girl often helped in distributing the letters. In an inn or in a home, letters were brought to be sent on their way and letters were claimed. Stage-coaches plied their routes on certain days and they carried the mail, when the roads were passable for traveling.

Before stamps were invented, letters were folded in a special way and sealed with sealing wax. No letter was secure unless sealed and the habit of using sealing wax continued into the 20th century, then as an ornament only. The sticks of wax came in various colors and gold was very popular. Small stampers were fashioned mostly of ivory with an initial, or with three initials, of the writer at the end. The wax was heated in a flame, and as it dripped the stamper impressed the initial.

Besides sealing wax, a necessary article was a sand shaker, or a sander, holding fine sand or finely cut steel, used to dry the ink after a letter had been written.

Letters have always played an important part in life, bringing both sad news and good news. Today's vast network of post offices and mail carriers is a far cry from that old Pennsylvania post-carrier who knitted mittens and stockings as he leisurely jogged along on horseback to his destination.

73

THE MUSIC OF COW BELLS

IS THERE ANYTHING AS MUSICAL TO THE EAR OF THE CITY DWELLER AS
the sound of a cow bell coming across the pasture! Such a contrast to the
harsh jangle and screeches of a city street. The sound comes from away
down by the brook that winds its way along beyond a stone wall. It
reaches you as you pause to listen. There is music in the bell. It may be
a big bell with deep tones or it may be a faint tinkle of a small bell. It
sounds with every motion of the cow as she steps along over hillocks and
over rocky places.

Have you seen sheep quietly grazing in a pasture, keeping a formation and following a leader? The leader always wears a bell around her
neck. It is a smaller bell than that of the cow's and it gives out a faint
tinkle, for the motion of the sheep is very slight as the drove slowly
moves along the fresh green grass. A still smaller bell is the one a mother
turkey wears. It is round instead of oblong like the animal bells and is
only two inches long. The mother turkey took her brood in those early
days hither and yon, through nearby pastures and swamps. Turkeys
caught cold easily from exposure and often the mother stepped upon one
of her brood.

Those days seem far back to some of us, and those musical sounds
are part of our memories of the time when we visited the country and
tramped through the pastures in search of blueberries, huckleberries, or
blackberries. As you wandered along absorbed in filling your pail, you
would not know there was any cow around until your ear caught the
music of the bell in the distance.

In my collection is a group of bells that once hung on the farm animals, some twenty-five of them. The heavy cow bells measure eight inches
long, some are smaller, while the sheep bells are half the size. The one
for the turkey is round and tiny as would have to be for such a slender
neck. There are two much-worn straps that went around the animal's

neck and from which the bells hung. The tone of any bell is caused by the size of the bell, the thickness of the metal, and the size of the clapper. No two bells are alike; some are brass and some are copper. Some are thicker than others, which makes a deeper tone.

Music of cowbells

There were three ways to make a bell. One was to take a narrow strip, bend it in the middle and fold it over. There must have been some sort of a mold although no one has ever mentioned one. The sides of the piece were riveted, the top being whole where it was bent over. Sometimes the strip was shaped to taper so that the top was narrower than the bottom. One cow bell was cut from a straight strip of iron and when it was bent over, the corners of the bend stuck out like ears. The top of that one is the same size as the bottom.

There are bells that were cut from two pieces of metal and riveted together across the top and down the sides. That would have been a longer job. Still another shape is that of a molded bell, all in one piece of metal with no seam. That must have been done on a block for it has four square edges and a square top.

The clapper is a short metal rod with a ball at the end. It was set in in two different ways; one way was to thrust it through the top of the bell and fasten it with a nut or a cotter pin—a pin that spreads open in two parts. The other way was to make a ring, solder it to the top of the inside, and fasten the clapper to that. Some were fastened with a second ring and others had a long enough clapper so it could be fastened to the ring at the top. A band at the top of the bell on the outside was added to hold the strap. Some bells have a wide band of metal, while others have a wide loop, some reaching from one edge to the other, while others have a short loop.

It did not take me long to find that there was an overtone in each bell. Each bell has one tone and an overtone that vibrates one third higher in the scale. Remember how we used to sing *Do Mi?* Every bell has a do mi. And every bell seems to have a different pitch. I suppose one could have bells that make harmony, a fact which bell ringers have found out. But the cow bell or a sheep bell was never made with the idea of striking a pitch. The reason that a cow bell sounds across the pasture is because of that "do mi." You do not have as much in a small sheep bell for there is little length for vibration. The deep tones of cow bells vibrate a long distance because of that overtone.

Wooden cow bells have been found. Metal could not be had by every man, so he resorted to wood. In foreign countries, wooden cow bells were used on such animals as the yak and the musk ox. These wooden bells were made from a block of wood, shaped like a tent, rounded at the top and longer than wide. Two ears protruded at the top with a hole in each ear in which a cord was tied onto a strap that went around the animal's neck. Holes were bored in each side to make vibrations. Mine has three holes in each side. It must have been a man with a musical understanding to know how to bore the holes, at a certain distance apart. The clapper of wood is shaped like a tear drop, pointed at the top and rounded and large at the bottom. Some were made with one clapper, others with two, and still others with three. Mine has two. They were tied in by stringing a cord through a hole in the top and fastening it with a knot. Each clapper has a separate cord. Can you imagine a wooden cow bell with thick sides, cut from a block of wood, making music? It has a surprisingly musical tone.

Our memory is a blessing. Play a few minutes with these animal bells and see yourself back in the pasture, perhaps frightened by a cow, perhaps watching a number of them coming across the scrub, wending their way down toward the brook. What wouldn't you give to be back picking blueberries again; great, big luscious ones, or those enormous wild blackberries that filled your basket in no time at all!

74

THE SEPTEMBER HARVEST

THE MONTH OF SEPTEMBER BRINGS US HARVEST TIME. WE HARVEST grains, gather our vegetables and fruits, and prepare for the winter ahead.

Nature gives us the Harvest moon in September, which when full remains at the same fullness for three consecutive nights. And the warm spell which returns in November has been called Indian Summer, for it was then that the Indians gathered their last lot of vegetables, before the cold frosts struck the land.

There are many signs we watch for as a forecast of the winter ahead; sayings that have come down the centuries. If the husks on the ears of corn are heavy, a hard winter is due; if the husks are not heavy, a mild winter follows. Nature cares for the birds by giving them a bountiful harvest of berries and nuts if a severe winter comes over the land. We hear it said that animals are given an extra heavy coat of fur for protection. One prediction seems to hold true, although a strange one—if a chipmunk carries its tail out straight, the coming winter will be severe. We always see his tail perfectly upright. Each locality seems to have observed its own forecasts and they follow as the day follows the night.

The 20th century has lost much of the romance of Harvest time. Great machines cut, bundle, or thresh the grains, saving man many hours of labor. In the old days, the grain was threshed on the barn floor by two men working together. Each had a flail, a long wooden handle to which was attached a smaller arm of wood that played freely on leather thongs or a cord. One man walked down the length of the barn in one direction while the other man walked in the opposite direction, each swinging his flail and beating the grain from the stalks. Then this was gathered into a huge splint or wooden basket shaped like a big scoop and called a winnower. It was taken to the barn door, balanced on the worker's knee, and jounced up and down, first on one knee and then on the other. This operation blew off the chaff, leaving the kernels. Threshing floors in Pennsylvania had slits between the floor boards, through which the grain fell into containers below.

The September harvest

Corn was the first grain to be sown, as knowledge of this was learned from the Indians. The kernels were ground in stone mortars and later in mills. The first mills were called quernes, two large cylindrical stones with radiating grooves, one placed upon the other and held by a central pivot. The upper stone turned upon the lower. At first this was done by a horse traveling around the stone, fastened by a harness to a long shaft that extended from the center pivot. Wind mills and water mills were invented in due time. Windmills were constructed with huge arms which the wind caught and turned about, while water mills had a huge paddle wheel with blades that caught the water and which forced the wheel to turn.

Rye meal was the next to be cultivated. Wheat followed after a few years although it did not ripen well in the beginning. Oats came the last, for this grain, too, did not grow very well. The Colonists had come from countries where these grains had been sown and they turned to the new land for the same living.

The pumpkin was the first vegetable grown and it was very popular. It was a wild fruit known by the Indians. For years, they had been using them, cutting them into pieces, drying them, and stringing them for the winter. Pumpkins were cooked in the oven; the top was cut off and filled with milk. There was pumpkin bread. The Indians boiled pumpkins with peas, beans, and corn. One writer wrote—perhaps with sarcasm and perhaps with a touch of bitterness:

> We have pumpkins at morning and pumpkins at noon,
> If it were not for pumpkins, we should be undone.

Squashes were native vegetables, having an Indian name with various spellings. But potatoes had a hard time in becoming a vegetable. The first crop in 1763 was only eight bushels and it was believed that if a man ate them every day, he would not live seven years. All that remained was burned in the belief that if cattle or horses ate them, they would die. Potatoes were carried back to England and grown in Ireland. Some Irish settlers carried them back to New Hampshire and from then on they were called Irish potatoes. The word came from the Spanish *potata*. The real American potato was a sweet potato in the South called *batata,* whence comes the name of tata or tater. We call it a spud because that was the name of the narrow spade which was used in digging up the potatoes.

It was a strange way that was followed in cooking the potatoes! Mix with butter, sugar, and grape juice; dates, lemons, mace, nutmeg, cinnamon, and pepper were added next; finally this was covered with a frosting of sugar. Where were the potatoes? The sweet potato that grew first in Carolina was roasted, boiled, made into puddings, into bread, and pancakes.

Beans were plentiful and the Indians baked them in earthen pots, deep in the ground in a fire hole, just as we bake them today in fireless cookers. Other vegetables were peas, parsnips, turnips, and carrots.

Wild fruits grew bountifully; huckleberries, blackberries, strawberries, gooseberries, and grapes. These were preserved in sugar, pound for pound, and put away in earthen crocks. Apples, pears, and quinces appeared soon after the settling of the new country, for the trees were brought over from across the water. These, too, were preserved in rich syrup.

It was a full harvest that the Colonists reaped, one and two centuries ago, of grains, vegetables, and fruits.

In the fall, at Harvest time, out in the fields we see the tall shocks of corn standing like sentinels. And golden pumpkins lie scattered about them.

In the early days before the appearance of silos, the stalks were stacked in the fields in such a way that the tassels acted like a canopy, protecting the stalks beneath them. Some of the early barns were built with a pit for the cut corn stalks. And then came the outside silo, where the cut stalks were forced up with a blower and taken out as needed from doors on three levels. One farmer did not have enough corn stalks to fill his silo, so he added cut-up millet. Still the silo was not full and he went to a cider mill and brought home enough apple pomace to finish the filling. That last caused fermentation which is necessary for the stalks for the winter months.

75

OUR FINE HERITAGE OF CORN

WHAT A FEAST OF CORN WE HAVE EACH FALL! WE CAN HARDLY WAIT for it to ripen. We eat it off the cob, cooked; we eat it cold off the cob, cut up in milk; in succotash with beans; in fritters dropped in deep fat; and thousands of ears are put into deep freeze units or canned for the winter. Every fall we look forward to that feast.

While we find the word corn mentioned in the Book of Genesis, the word meant a cereal like wheat, oats, or barley. The corn we are familiar with today is of purely American origin. It originally was called maize or Indian corn since it was introduced to the Colonists by the Indians, who used it for a staple food. The Indians made a porridge from the kernels, ground coarsely and boiled in water. That they called samp. The mortar in which the kernels were ground was tall with a shallow cavity. Pestles were stone. Powdered kernels were used as food and it was claimed that five spoonfuls a day would sustain a person. The Colonists survived on that ration of powdered kernels in time of drought.

The kernels were ground for meal, first in stone or wooden mortars and later crushed between two millstones by horse power or by windmills. The meal was cooked in water and made into mush, often called hasty pudding. Hasty pudding belied its name, for it required a long, slow cooking in those big iron kettles. Who hasn't enjoyed a bowl of mush and milk or mush and maple syrup! How tasty and appetizing hasty pudding is when it is fried in thin slices and eaten with maple syrup!

Corn bread we bake today, sometimes in a pan, sometimes in the old iron muffin pans. It used to be called Johnny cake and it still goes by that name. It took the name because the cakes were carried on the midwinter trips or journeys to market. The name shortened from journey cake to jonny cake and we say Johnny cake. In the South, the cakes were called hoe cakes because the pats of coarse stiff dough were baked on the head of a hoe, placed before the fire. In the North they were first called

Our fine heritage of corn

bannock cakes, because they were baked on a board propped up against a kettle or on a rest of its own. The board was called a bannock board. The name originally came from Scotland, spelled *bonnach* and the cakes were made of oatmeal or barley and baked on a griddle. Each nationality brought over their ways of living and their old names, which seemed to cling for more than one generation.

We still make Indian Pudding and brown bread with part Indian meal, which we serve with our Saturday's baked beans.

The fun of popping corn has been sold out to the paper bag industry. Many of us still pop corn before an open fire or over a flame and we butter and salt it and eat it plain or in milk. We make pop corn molasses balls. Today's younger generations only know buttered pop corn or molasses cakes as something that is packaged and easily bought, with the generous weekly allowance which they carry around.

The hulled corn man does not come around the neighborhood any more. He used to carry it in a wooden bucket and scoop it out into one of your dishes. Hulled corn was prepared by boiling the kernels in a weak solution of lye and then drying them.

Corn gives to man as much as any other vegetable or grain. The stalks were used when dry as thatch for roofs. They were cut and used for fuel in some sections and the stalks were shredded and used in making baskets. In years past, the long leaves were dried for fodder and today a variety of field corn is grown and cut into fodder by machinery for cattle.

Chemists have known the science of extracting starch from corn stalks and we can buy starch for the laundry and corn starch for puddings.

The husks around the ears were used for various purposes. Remember the braided husk mats at the side door in the country farm house? Those were made from dried husks, and whenever they wore out new ones were made. They were tough and the 1½-inch-wide braid made a mat of long service. The romance of those mats has captivated the modern generations and the mats are being made today in several localities.

Dried husks were used as stuffing for chairs and saddles and bed mattresses. Chopped or shredded fine with a hetchel that was used to clean flax, they made a durable stuffing; but a mattress was not as comfortable as might be expected.

We children used to play with the silk tassel of the ear of corn. It made a wonderful imitation of hair or a moustache. And in all country stores there were corn cob pipes made from a piece of the cob, shellacked, with a pipe stem inserted. The silk tassle could be dried and smoked in the pipe. The boys used to try that on the sly!

Every late summer and into the fall we look forward to the season when we can sit down to a meal of tender, golden ears. And we always have on hand Indian meal for mush and cakes. How thankful we are for this bountiful heritage.

76

INDIAN SUMMER COMES IN NOVEMBER

WHENEVER A FEW WARM DAYS COME IN THE FALL OF THE YEAR, YOU hear, "This is Indian Summer!" It is in our conversation, over the radio, and written in print, "Indian Summer."

The autumnal equinox, or in common language the fall, begins approximately September 22nd. The days change perceptibly beginning in another week and we have cool days and warm days, frosty nights and warm nights. We are then due for a glorious month of October with clear skies, a tang in the air, and gorgeous coloring in the foliage. All this is rightly called fall, several weeks of perfect weather before Winter comes to our minds.

Later on, in November, there comes a smoky or hazy appearance in the atmosphere, especially near the horizon. This is caused by the decay and slow chemical combustion of leaves, grass, and other vegetable matter, whenever there is frost at night and a warm sun in the daytime. This does not take place until November, after continued frosty nights.

Long years ago, the early settlers attributed this haze and smoky appearance in November to the fires kindled by the Indians in their villages. The settlers talked about this warm period and gave it the name of Indian Summer.

It was in this last warm period, around the second week of November, that the Indians instinctively saw the signs of the approaching winter and began laying in their stores of food; their corn and vegetables, and the strips of meat called jerk meat, which they had sun-dried. The Indians were not good providers and either ate all of their harvest before cold weather came or else waited until this last warm spell before finishing the harvest. They often had to ask for food from the settlers in exchange for pelts. The settlers watched the Indians lay in their stores of food and called that warm spell the Indian's Summer.

269

Indian Summer comes in November

So we have two indisputable reasons why Indian Summer comes in November and not before. The warm days of October are merely a continuation of a late summer. And we can be glad that we are due one final spell in November before we think of winter.

77

STONE WALLS AND FENCES

THOUSANDS OF TOURISTS FROM ALL OVER THE COUNTRY SEE NEW England in the summer; some are seeing it for the first time, others are returning to their home towns. There is nothing that makes such an indelible impression on their minds as the green pastures, hemmed in by stone walls or fences. Some are grazing lands, others are making hay for the barns. The green verdure of spring and summer presents a picture even up to late July and August when the haying season begins.

New England is famous for its pastures and stone walls. It was a rocky land that confronted the Pilgrim Fathers and those rocks and stones were of necessity put to use, as foundations for buildings and boundaries for pastures. Rocks and boulders were moved by oxen and then put onto stone drags and taken into a cellar hole to make a foundation. Seeing some of those foundations when exploring old houses makes one realize the size of those boulders and the difficulty the workers had in putting them into place. So, too, in making a stone wall that was to last through the years, huge boulders were laid as a foundation with the aid of oxen and a stone drag. Stone walls still continue to mark off many pastures but more and more stones are being taken and used in road beds. Perhaps some day we shall see the passing of the stone walls as we are seeing the passing of the covered bridges.

Fences appeared as soon as those first families settled in the various sections. In the beginning, a central Common was fenced off for the cows, each owner of a herd taking the responsibility for his share of 20 feet of fence for each cow he had pastured. He had to keep it in repair. Fence-viewers were appointed to watch the condition of the fences. Gardens and grain were fenced in, with geese and swine roaming at will; in later years the barnyard fowl and the four-footed animals were restrained.

271

Stone walls and fences

Fences in themselves are interesting. Up here in New England, there were so many ways of making those boundary lines for pastures. One of the fences that required no fastenings was called a "lazy man's fence." This was made by laying the end of one rail upon the end of another at more than a 45 degree angle. Each rail was laid upon the end of the other up to the required height. The opposite ends were then laid upon the next set of rails, one at a time, that set again making an angle, which formed a zig-zag formation. One such rail which I photographed, even in disrepair, lies in the fields in Greenfield, Massachusetts. A few are spied as we drive through the country towns, covered with wild growth or rotted away.

There is the split rail fence for which Lincoln became famous. It is claimed that he learned that from his ancestors in Hingham. Posts were driven into the ground at regular distances. Each post had four or five slots, into which a rail would be set. When necessary to have an opening, the rails or bars could very easily be let down. Such a fence as a boundary to the property of Ford's wayside Inn can be seen on the old Post Road running from Worcester to Boston.

It was not uncommon to see a low stone wall topped by rails for extra height, generally laid onto short crotched rails. Barbed wire was often added to stone walls for more height and protection.

In some sections of the country, stumps that had been pulled up when trees were cut were placed as a boundary line for a pasture. There were often so many stumps to dispose of, it would be a sensible way to use them for fencing in cattle.

Board fences appeared around barns, out buildings, and houses. They gave much protection in their height. That was in the time when wood was plentiful. When it became more and more scarce, wire and barbed wire was used, fastened to posts. Today, this wire is often electrified to prevent cattle from going astray.

How much it means to belong to New England! We take it for granted if we have always lived here. But let us look around us this summer and see our green pastures and our stone walls. Or, if we do not journey, we have our memories, reaching back to childhood, of those green pastures with their stone walls and fences.

78

MAN HAS LONG BLAZED TRAILS

BOSTON WAS ONE OF THE FIRST CITIES FOUNDED AFTER THE LANDING of the Pilgrims at Plymouth—spelled *Plimoth*. The ocean went far inland in those first years, gradually receding as time went on. There were no streets, merely lanes, following the paths made by cows as they wound their way to and from the Common. Boston's Common was the large central plot of land, which still remains the same today. It was common property to all the townspeople who had cows to pasture; whence it derived the name of Common.

Each owner of cows was responsible for a certain portion of the fence which bounded the common, twenty feet for each cow he had pastured. All of the cows were branded by their owners, or had a special cutting in their ears, called "ear marks." A man was appointed as cow-herd, taking the cows to the Common in the early morning and leading them home at twilight. Ralph Waldo Emerson was at one time cow-herd, when he had but recently married and lived in Boston. He would start through the paths leading to the Common, blowing his horn for the cows to follow. The cow paths led from all directions.

Peddlers, called pack peddlers because of the packs on their backs, followed those cow paths and went their way selling goods. Gradually the paths widened and could be used by men on horseback. In time, they became roads and traveling radiated in many directions, so that wagons and coaches could make trips up North to Concord, New Hampshire, South to the Coastal towns, and West to New York.

Worcester came in for its share of those roads when stagecoaches began to run from Boston to New York. The roads were not always passable and traveling was done only of necessity. Through mud, tangles of underbrush, and dense wooded sections, the road wound its way at its own will. The history of those stagecoaches and those days gives an accurate-picture of the towns and highways as they were first made by man.

Cattle, sheep, and turkeys were driven to a selling market, traveling those cow paths which had widened in time to roads. Imagine the long, slow journey, stopping at dusk, putting the cows into pasture, and then off at sunrise the next morning. Sheep, too, were taken to market over the roads. It must have been a queer sight to see turkeys on their way to market. They flew up into trees as the day came to a close. In the morning, down they dropped and off they strutted for another day's journey.

Population increased, cities sprung up, business broadened, and soon the roads became streets and thoroughfares. Traveling on foot gave way to horseback and stagecoaches. The locomotive was conceived, the horsecar appeared, and the roads led from one town to another, from one state to another.

Man has long blazed trails

By the twentieth century, the automobile took over; and now everything has been keyed up to meet the rapid progress of traveling. Highways have been made and cities have become radiating centers. Superhighways of six lanes have been made as networks, stretching across the country. Toll roads have been built. To meet the demands of the increasing number of automobiles, cities have planned "arteries," cutting through old residential sections. And toll roads have taken away homes and farms.

The Indians bent trees for trails, the white man followed footpaths. The mechanical age brings superhighways and toll roads, reaching across the country.

79

WITH SCYTHE AND SWITCHEL

OLD DAYS AND OLD WAYS ARE GONE FOREVER. BUT MUSEUMS AND collectors are keeping those ways alive by their collections of early hand tools.

I have a strange piece of woodenware. It would be unnamed still if the finder had not been told for what purpose it was made. It is shaped like a cylinder of pine, 10½ inches long, 2½ inches in diameter, and tapered to a point at the bottom. It is hollow, a cavity of six inches. It was once painted green but it was scraped to its natural color. At one side of the upper edge, there are two small holes. Into these were tied two short loops of strong cord. To these loops, two larger cords were tied, measuring a yard and a half long.

When a man went into the hay field, he took along his whetstone with his scythe. It was very important that the scythe have a keen edge for cutting long grass. It was also important that the whetstone be dipped into water before it was used to sharpen the blade of the scythe. There was a knack to using the whetstone, making long graceful strokes, first on one side and then on the other.

Often a field that was to be mowed had no access to a brook or pond. Some creative farmer thought out a way of having water for his whetstone when he made this wooden holder. He tied it around his waist with the cord, filled it with water, and put in the whetstone. When he reached the field, he took off the holder and stuck the pointed end into the ground. There it was whenever it was time to sharpen the scythe.

It was an art to swing the scythe, to have the arms and body in perfect rhythm as the worker cut his swathe. It is a lost art, and with the coming of the mowing machine, the scythe has almost passed into history.

Besides taking the holder with water for the whetstone, the farmer took a keg of switchel down into the fields. Or perhaps, one of the women

With scythe and switchel

brought it down at noontime. There were many kinds of kegs and everyone drank out of the bung hole. One keg had triangular-shaped ends and
was carried by a cord fastened to the edge of each end. That was called
a rundlet. Others were barrel shaped, carried by leather straps. Still another was called a swigler. It was a hollowed-out piece of wood, four or
five inches in diameter, with solid ends to make it water-tight. Stoppers
were always shaped pieces of wood. The swigler was so named because
it held one long swig, for one man.

Switchel was water sweetened with molasses. Sometimes, ginger, nutmeg, and vinegar were added. That made a tasty, refreshing drink. Sometimes a handful of oatmeal was put into water, which became slightly
fermented as it stood in the keg. Haying on hot days was hard work and
the men needed refreshment.

80

SOLD TO THE HIGHEST BIDDER

IF YOU HAVE MISSED OUT GOING TO AUCTIONS, YOU HAVE MISSED ONE
of the most interesting times you could have. It is an education plus recrea-
tion plus fun. You may not be a bit interested in antiques or in buying
anything, but what a thrill you can have from being one of the crowd
that goes to auctions!

There are auctions and auctions, to be sure. The aristocratic auction
is the one that is always held under a tent, with floodlights. Chairs are
set out as if for a show and there are plenty of them. There is a platform
and a high desk, like a throne with a fancy cloth covering it, at which the
auctioneer sits or stands. There are two people who handle the change
box and there are three or four helpers or bus boys who hold the pieces
being auctioned, take them to the bidders, and make the change. There
is little conversation among the group for they listen attentively and do
not miss any of the prices or the remarks that are made.

Another kind of auction is the one held by the back door of a house
or at the big barn door. You must have your own camp chair or be out
of luck. People crowd in front of you or push you behind, standing or
walking around. Children and dogs run everywhere. Even baby carriages
with crying babies are in evidence. Everyone seems to want to talk, to
visit, to compare notes; and the poor auctioneer cries his stuff above the
din. Often he becomes desperate and asks for quiet. Once on a terribly
hot day, with no air stirring, the auctioneer called out, "If you people
would stop talking and I stopped hollering, we would be a lot cooler!"

Another kind of auction is carried on with a very serious attitude.
Everything to be sold is in a barn or shed and the auctioneer stands on a
box in front, selling off one lot after another. Old tools, old kitchen stuff,
broken-down furniture, cracked and chipped china and glass—it all goes
for a price. Somebody wants something. The crowd stands and presses
closer and closer, to be where they can see things as they come out. They

stand on boxes, trunks, or old chairs, eagerly awaiting a chance to buy something to take home—probably to be thrown out later!

If an auctioneer cannot provoke good humor with quips, jokes, and stories, he is pretty dull. He has to be good and he has to have the crowd with him and he has to know how to make a bidder go on and up. Then most likely, the bidder will exclaim, "Why did I bid on that when it is cracked!" One auctioneer of more or less renown brings much emotion into his sales. "Think of the dear Grandma who made this beautiful quilt! Every piece that went into it came from a dress or shirt or apron. All her love and her time went into it. Just think!"

At one auction, an old melodeon was brought out of the house. No one seemed inclined to make a bid. "Who'll play for us?" the auctioneer cried. A young man came forward and began to play an old song. Before you could say Jack Robinson, the crowd joined in singing. Then the bids began to come. "Play another song" came from the auctioneer. We joined in a second song, an old folk song. The melodeon went for a good price.

Sold to the highest bidder

Things are often lumped together at these country auctions and you have to take trash along with what you are bidding on. I bought a large splint cheese basket once, filled with boxes of nails, screws, hardware, and two crane hooks for the fireplace. I wanted just the basket. At lunch time, I saw two farmers bending over my basket. They wanted to buy the stuff that was in it. I sold the nails, screws, and hardware and then found my basket and crane hooks had cost me just 15 cents! The farmers got a bargain and I got what I wanted.

Another time, I wanted a large wooden plate, a very rare piece. Only one bidder beside myself called out, so the auctioneer grabbed an empty bird cage, slapped it onto the plate, and said, "How much!" I had to take the plate with the bird cage. Someone standing by me said, "Isn't that lovely, that bird cage! They put it over a plant and it's real pretty!" "Want it for a quarter?" was my come-back. My plate cost me that much less. I saw the other bidder after the auction and asked him why he stopped bidding. "The darn thing was cracked!" Yes, it was cracked on the rim and mended with a piece of tow, laced through holes made by an augur. A collector of woodenware prizes far more anything that shows thrift, something recovered after long usage. Collectors of glass or china cannot buy an imperfect piece, they cannot know how families lived, worked, and saved when there is no sign of usage.

If you do not get something out of an auction, you are not human. Go alone or go with a friend or the family. Take a lunch if you are particular or buy a hot dog, a cup of coffee, and a slab of pie at the stand—somebody is always on hand with a car of refreshments. Talk and joke with this stranger or that and find out what a lot of nice people there are at an auction. Before you realize it, you will be buying something and you will begin to collect something. You will know then the full joy of living.

Next time you see a red flag flying from a tree when you are out riding, stop. A red flag means an auction. Don't miss it! Summer goes, but auctions go on all the year.

81

WEATHER COCKS ARE NO MORE

A FRIEND OF MINE HAS A RARE COLLECTION OF WEATHERVANES. YOU might wonder how anyone could collect such large pieces, but her den is well adapted to hold them. Two built-in bookcases either side of a door-way, with a wide top, hold two of them, a third one is on a wide mantle, and a fourth is suspended on a wall.

The two weathervanes on the bookcases and the one on the mantle are wheeled vehicles, about four feet long. Two are racers, one having four wheels and the other two wheels. The jockey has a coat and cap and holds a whip. The horse shows great speed and the facial expression of the jockey shows an intense strain, as he holds onto his wire reins. The two-wheeled racer is a sulky. In both of the racers the men and horses were made double to represent two dimensions, breadth as well as length. The two pieces were soldered together, each being a duplicate of the other. The vehicles, wheels, spokes, and shafts are single sheets of metal. These two racing vehicles were once on barns, with the four direction arms, N. E. S. W.

Perhaps the most interesting and complete one of the collection is a fire vehicle. It carries a frame at the back of two wheels on which is wound the fire hose. Two hatchets are fastened to the side. It was found on a fire house, as was most natural. This was made with double man and horse; all else is single. With it at one time were the four points of the compass.

A fourth weathervane on the wall represent Sagittarius, a centaur, half man and half horse. His bow in the arrow points the direction of the winds, with no other arms of the compass needed. The body is a single sheet while the arms and feet are double. It is about 4 feet high and 4 feet long and very striking.

A later addition is a minister in a long coat and high hat riding on a high-wheel bicycle. Some day, more acquisitions will be added!

Weather cocks of yesterday

A weathervane owned by another collector is in the shape of a plow. The plowshare is shaped realistically, the end pointing the direction of the wind. This is about 4 feet long and 3 feet high, with both single and double parts. Such a weathervane has appeared on barns today.

A rare weathervane of wood came to my attention at an Antique Show. It was a gray goose, made solid of wood, 4 feet long and 2 feet high. It had a light gray body and dark gray wings—a beautiful and natural goose. This now reposes in a public Village Museum.

We find the first mention of a weathercock at the time of the Romans, on a steeple. Pope Nidadas in the middle of the 9th century ordained that a figure of a cock should surmount every church throughout Christendom, to remind people that Jesus said that Peter would deny him at the cockcrow, when the cock crowed thrice. Chaucer mentions a weathercock in the 14th century: "he was a wedercock that turneth his face with every wind." Then Shakespeare in the 16th century tells of the rain that "drenched over steeples, drowned the cocks." Longfellow in the 19th century writes that the "noisy weathercocks rattled and sang of mutation."

With the figure of a cock were 4 arms to point the direction of the wind, N. E. S. W., set below the cock.

Although first placed on steeples, the cock was later put onto barns. Most barns had cupolas for ventilation and the weathercock was put on top. Because there were so many barns in the early days, the weathercocks were common and they represented many things. Farmers lived by the turn of the weathercocks, adjusting their day's work by the direction of the winds.

When weathercocks became numerous, in the 18th and 19th century, the name changed to weathervanes. No longer was it limited to a cock. It was made to represent other barnyard animals, such as a cow, a sheep, a horse, a dog, or even an eagle. The cow and the horse were the most common. On the coast, it was a fish and on a tobacco plantation, a tobacco leaf. Other figures gradually appeared.

Weathervanes were made of brass or copper which did not rust from exposure. They were gilded to catch the changing lights. The animals were double and hollow, made of two identical pieces riveted or soldered together. They were large, often measuring 4 and 5 feet long or high and were perfect facsimiles of the animal.

There are not many old weather-cocks today. The new barns do not boast of them and the old barns have lost their cupolas while the weather vanes that set on top have gone to collectors. Copies are being made of the old, and arrows are popular, pointing the direction of the winds, on steeples as well as barns. Weather predictions are given in detail in the daily paper and over the radio and television, but we have lost the art of predicting for ourselves as we watch the turn of the weather vane. Weather cocks and weather vanes are gone with the past, lingering only in our memories.

82

THE BLACKSMITH WAS A VERY IMPORTANT MAN

OFTEN MY MIND GOES BACK TO MY CHILDHOOD WHEN OUR FAMILY VACA-
tioned in Paxton, a little town north of Worcester. Up in town there was
a blacksmith shop. Many times when we children went to the Post Office
for the mail we would stop at the blacksmith shop. We would stand in
the big wide door and then we would venture in.

We were fascinated as we watched the blacksmith pump the big bellows and make the fire burn more furiously. A piece of iron was heating,
and when it was white hot the blacksmith took it out with his big tongs,
placed it on his anvil, and pounded it until it began to take shape—for
a horseshoe, an andiron, or other necessities for the home. How the sparks
flew and how the anvil rang out as the iron was being struck!

Sometimes we would see a horse being shod. The horse could lift one
foot at a time as the blacksmith held it between his knees on his leather
apron. Not so with an ox. An ox cannot stand on three legs to have the
fourth shod. His weight is too heavy for his slender legs and feet. There
has to be apparatus consisting of a leather sling and ropes and pulleys.
The ox is lifted in the sling as one foot after the other is shod. Everyone knows how a horseshoe looks but it was many years before I knew
the shape of a shoe for an ox. It is narrow and curved for oxen have
cloven hoofs and the shoe is fastened to the outside part only.

The blacksmith appeared in early history and was considered a man
of high rank. It was he who fashioned the implements for war, and because of that he was carefully guarded lest he be captured by the enemy.

It was the blacksmith who fashioned from iron the many necessities
for the home—nails, shovels, pokers, tongs, kettles, and more. He riveted,
he welded, and he shaped into form.

There is a blacksmith shop standing as if but recently vacated in a
town some distance from Worcester. The building still has its old red
paint. Within is all the equipment necessary for a blacksmith, dating back

more than 100 years ago. A forge, with bellows and hood overhead, a huge anvil and long benches with tools seem to await the return of the blacksmith. A rare piece is a frame for making hoops for buckets and barrels. It stands a tall, tapering cylinder of wood, four feet high. Each hoop took its own diameter as it was placed around the cylinder, from the small one at the top for a bucket to the large one at the bottom for a barrel. The iron bands were riveted after being set for size.

The blacksmith was a very important man

A flight of stairs leads to a loft above where there are parts of carriages, sleighs, wheels, and other useless truck. Besides the big wide door, there are two smaller doors leading out into the yard and into the street that leads to the town. Very little light enters through the small panes of glass that are covered with cobwebs and dust of the passing years. Light must have come from the big door and the fierce fire that was kept burning with the bellows. Now the shop stands idle, a mute evidence of the important blacksmith that worked at his forge.

So much is lost for the children of today to experience and learn. Horses, oxen, and blacksmith shops are now only memories of the older generations.

83

SPRINGTIME IS SHEEP SHEARING TIME

COLLECTORS ARE FUNNY PEOPLE. WHEN WE GO SEARCHING FOR A PIECE, we so often run across something strange about which we know nothing. And then curiosity gets the better of us; we buy it, take it home, and find out its history and background afterwards. This has often happened to me in my collecting.

Once I found two sheep stamping blocks of wood, with the owner's initials cut deep into them, all smeared with a tarry substance. It was a lucky find but I knew nothing about sheep or how they were stamped. I wanted to know.

Sheep often numbered up to 16,000 in a community. Each sheep was marked by its owner for identification, the stamping done with wood blocks, either with numbers or initials. The block was dipped in a tarry substance and imprinted onto the flesh when the shearing was done. Then as the wool began to grow, the stamp moved along with it until it ap-

Springtime is sheep shearing time

peared on the outer edge. The sheep were led into a brook to be washed and many were the cockle burrs and brambles.

Shearing time was from the first of May through the middle of July. Raising sheep for wool was important in New England, Pennsylvania, New York, and Virginia. Nantucket turned the time into a holiday, lasting two or more days. A sheep fold was built in a pasture about two miles from town, tents were erected, and a platform for dancing was built. The day the shearing took place, a veritable feast was laid out on tables, for all to enjoy. Such occasions became community gatherings, with everyone helping and sharing in the dancing, singing, and eating.

Sheep shearers had to be vary skillful and avoid nipping the flesh. After each sheep was shorn of its heavy coat, the body was wrapped in straw, lest it take cold and die of exposure. Some breeds of sheep produced up to 30 pounds of wool each. The average supplied between five and ten pounds.

Today, the sheep are being marked in a different way. Each sheep has a plastic tag attached to its ear with a number or name. An early custom of marking cows in this country was by cutting the ear in some special way to denote ownership. From this came the expression "earmarks."

Cleaning and sorting the wool was a long process. Short hair was separated from the best. Then came the long work of dyeing and carding, preparing the wool for spinning. Young girls and mothers and grandmothers took a hand at the weaving. Sometimes the wool was dyed after the weaving was done. That brought about the expression "dyed in the wool." Another old saying was "all wool and a yard wide" because the loom was made for yard-wide cloth when finished. All the clothing of the entire family was made from wool, even the stockings and gloves. It was many years before sheep became numerous enough to be slaughtered for meat and for tallow, which was used in making candles. The wool was more important.

A flock of sheep grazing will always be led by one, to all appearances a born leader. Sheep graze in formation, moving along and keeping the formation. The leader wore a bell on a leather strap, as those bells in my collection testify.

Today, many families boast of one or two sheep from which the wool is taken for blankets. The owner is rightly proud of his blanket!

84

WHEN STRAW WAS A NEW ENGLAND STANDBY

ONE NIGHT, MY MOTHER TOLD ME ABOUT HER GOING IN A STAGECOACH to see her Grandpa in the neighboring town. Her recollection as a little child was very vivid—climbing up the high steps, sitting in the back seat with her feet in straw that covered the floor of the stagecoach.

Straw! What a necessary commmodity it was in those early days! And even to the present time. It was nothing but the waste part of grain after it had been threshed on the barn floor. Wheat, oats, barley, and rye—all had that covering, that waste. But it was not wasted.

Imagine the discomfort of a straw mattress! Homespun ticking was made into a bag or tick and that was filled with straw. Whenever a new mattress was needed, there was plenty of new stuffing lying handy. There were three grades of mattresses. The best was filled with down from the geese, the next in grade was filled with feathers from wild birds, and the third was filled with straw. The best went onto the bed of the mistress of the family, the next went to the children, and the last to servants and the wandering tinkers and peddlers. When stagecoach drivers stopped at a tavern to sleep their allotted time, their accommodations were pretty meager. Often it was a bunk covered with straw, made slightly more comfortable with homespun blankets. If a mattress was offered, it was of straw.

Never a stagecoach went from East to West or North to South but what it had straw at the feet of its passengers. And never a sleigh left the barn but what it had straw on the floor. It helped keep the feet warm when temperatures dropped.

In the barn, cattle and horses were bedded down with straw. It was a daily task to keep it fresh and to toss it lightly into place.

Even the housewife found straw a standby. Whenever she fried her sausage cakes in deep fat in her iron kettle, she laid them on straw to drain. Straw absorbed the extra grease. And when she made apple butter,

When straw was a New England standby

she often resorted to a layer of straw at the bottom of the kettle to keep the mess from burning. It took a hot fire to make the butter.

Up in the attic, the housewife had her supply of maple molasses for her cooking. It was kept for the long winter in a barrel. In place of a spigot or stopper, a twist of straw was inserted in the bung hole. That kept out the ants and allowed the air to enter so the molasses would not sour.

Do you remember the straw rides we used to have? The long wagon was either on wheels or on runners and it was pulled by two big farm horses. The bottom of the wagon was covered with a deep layer of straw which made a warm and soft place for the jolly crowd of young people. Plenty of buffalo robes were needed for a winter's night ride.

By another generation, straw matting for floor covering was very popular. How well we grownups remember the bedrooms and hallways that were laid with straw matting! That did not come from the threshing floor but from Canton, China. It made a clean-looking room with a peculiar clean-smelling odor. But when the matting was taken up to be renewed, we found it was anything but a clean floor covering. Straw has been plaited for centuries for hats for men, women, and children, imported from other countries.

It was a rare New England family indeed that did not make use of the straw, the waste, that was threshed from wheat, oats, barley, and rye.

85

THE BIRTH OF THE HAMMOCK

IN ONE OF THE NARRATIVES OF COLUMBUS, DESCRIBING HIS LANDING on the coast of the West Indies, he relates how "a great many Indians in canoes came to the ship today for the purpose of bartering their cotton and hamacas or nets in which they sleep." *Hamaca* is a Spanish word whence came our hammock. They were called nets because they were woven of coarse twine or cord made from hemp.

In the Gay Nineties, the rope hammock was the common thing out in the back yard. It swung between two trees, for yards in those days had plenty of shade trees. A curved stick about 3 feet long, the size of a broomstick, came with the hammock. Fastened in it were 6 or 8 bent headless nails. The stick was put in at the head of the hammock, the nails catching in the ropes, spreading out the hammock full width. Then a pillow could be put in and that made a comfortable place to relax.

We had such a net hammock in our back yard, between a maple tree and the corner of the house. That maple tree was planted when it had three leaves and Mother watered it every day. Now it has grown to be far above our big house and has been cabled and trimmed countless times. It would show rings of 80 years or more. The hammock hook eventually disappeared when the tree grew and covered it with the years' growth.

Rough handling such as children gave a string hammock could not hurt it. We used to wrap ourselves all up in the hammock and one of the children would turn us over and over, upside down and rightside up! Such fun are memories of the older generations today!

A better kind of hammock came next, made of loosely woven cloth. It came in colors with stripes of orange, black, and yellow. These had side pieces that hung down with fringe. At the head was a bolster, made into the hammock, holding it out about the width of a yard. These hammocks were very popular and every family had one or even two. Sometimes they were swung on a porch. The rope that held the hammocks had to be watched, for in time they wore out and the hammock broke down.

The birth of the hammock

It was really a bad jolt when the rope broke, and not always a laughable matter!

An early home-made hammock was one made of slats, woven together with a heavy cord. These came onto the market. They could take hard wear but had to be supplied with old quilts or blankets for comfort.

Gradually shade trees disappeared from the back yard. The yard became a nice lawn with large flower gardens, berry bushes, and great mounds of rhubarb. Croquet on such a spacious lawn was most popular but finally disappeared along with the swinging hammock.

A canvas hammock was made for the piazza with sides and back of canvas and a spring and mattress. That could take rough handling, but it was not easy to pile up pillows and be comfortable.

Then came the glider. That was made like a living room divan with three separate cushions and three back cushions, on a heavy iron frame. You could swing in it or glide gently back and forth. It was a lot of work to set up the glider in the spring and take it down in the fall. And a lot of work, too, to keep it covered in the quick thunderstorms and at night. The final development was the chaise longue, with wheels so that it might be placed in any part of the piazza. Inner springs are in the mattress and the back is adjustable. It is a colorful addition to any piazza, with its gayly colored plastic covering and white enamel parts.

Hammocks are back again, sold with a frame in which they hang. They can be used out in the yard or on a piazza. They swing low, nearly to the ground, and it is a difficult feat for those of the older generation to get into it or to get out of it. Gone are the hammocks that swing between two trees out in the yard, where the sun shines and the breeze wafts fragrant odors.

EPILOGUE: AGE WILL COME

Age will come to all of us—
  It comes to everyone;
It comes in all its glory
  As sure as setting sun.

Some grow old so early—
  They do not reach afar;
They settle down in sad, sad ways,
  They lose their wee small star.

Each one of us should have a star,
  Something to guide our way;
Something to lead us on and on,
  Giving us strength each day.

When age comes on, as it surely will,
  What have we got to say?
Can we face it and still have courage,
  Can we give of ourselves each day?

I like to think as I count the years,
  I have given of the best of my life;
I like to think as I face my age,
  I have met head-on the strife.

The friends I've made—such true, true friends,
  They love me as I was meant to be;
I gave myself, I shared my all—
  As age comes on, so you shall see.

Mary Earle Gould
Worcester, Massachusetts
1967

INDEX